The AMERICAN BOULANGERIE

The AMERICAN BOULANGERIE

French Pastries and Breads for the Home Kitchen

PASCAL RIGO
and the Bakers of Bay Bread

Foreword by
CAROL FIELD

Photography by
PAUL MOORE

Produced by
TINA SALTER

Text © 2003 by Pascal Rigo
Foreword © 2003 by Carol Field
Photography © 2003 by Paul Moore
(excluding photographs on pages 2 and 4)

Library of Congress Cataloging-in-Publication data is
on file with the Publisher.

ISBN 1-57959-527-8
Printed and bound in China

10 9 8 7 6 5 4 3 2 1

Distributed to the trade by Publishers Group West

Bay Books is an imprint of BAY/SOMA Publishing,
444 De Haro St., No.130
San Francisco, California 94107
www.baybooks.com

For BAY/SOMA Publishing:
Publisher: James Connolly
Editorial Director: Floyd Yearout

Producer/Editor: Tina Salter
Photographer: Paul Moore
Photographer's Assistant: Jeff McLain
Designer: Catherine Jacobes Design
Writer: Steve Siegelman
Food and Prop Stylist: George Dolese
Recipe Editor: Christine Swett
Copyeditor: Carolyn Krebs
Indexer: Ken DellaPenta

A mes parents,
Micheline et Jean Rigo, who let me do what I loved—
and encouraged me, all the way to the end...

Thank you to my wonderfully supportive wife, Virginie,
and my children Juliette, Pauline, and Oscar.
You are the jewels of my life.

CONTENTS

FOREWORD *by Carol Field*

FIRST THERE WAS THE BUZZ, THEN THE BLUE DOOR, and finally the bakery with the sign that said simply Boulangerie. From the beginning crowds spilled out the door, a large number of them French speaking. And no wonder: they had entered what looked like an authentic French bakery with flour-veiled wheels of rustic *pain au levain*, fat walnut baguettes, buttery almond paste-filled croissants, *epis* shaped like leaves on a branch, and glazed brioche loaves. Canvas-lined bakers' baskets perched on the case tops offered tastes of breads, lemon cake, *pain au chocolat*.

All this in my neighborhood! The crowds grew larger and the buzz got louder as new products filled the glass cases: baby *tartes tatin*; *cannelés de Bordeaux* with their crunchy caramelized exteriors; rustic pear and apple tarts; croissant bread pudding, Proustian madeleines, Parisian macaroons flavored with cassis, hazelnuts, or cafe.

In no time the bakery became a neighborhood institution. More people kept arriving, no doubt drawn by word of mouth and by the smell of breads and pastries being made in the large open section just beyond the selling area. Everyone could look in and see loaves being pulled from the ovens and watch savory and sweet tarts cooling on racks. The crew never stopped. When baskets were empty, they were filled again, as the bakers produced a second and third bake.

Obviously such a place doesn't just appear on its own. Behind the seemingly endless supply of bread and pastry is a man who says he is making his dream come true. Pascal Rigo, a Frenchman with startling blue eyes, began baking when he was a boy in Bordeaux and now lives over the store with his family—easily spotted in his beige shorts and tennis shoes, his deep tan and muscular frame, moves between upstairs and down and can sometimes be spotted in deep conversation with one of the bakers.

What Pascal started a mere four years ago as a small neighborhood bakery has since grown into a small empire that includes three bakery/cafes and three restaurants as well as a commissary kitchen that bakes for a chain of markets and for the city's best French-accented restaurants. He has recently made arrangements with three artisan bakeries in Paris for employees to spend time learning the authentic ways of French baking.

For someone who thinks of himself as a baker at heart, Pascal acts like an entrepreneur who keeps creating jobs and as an impassioned idea-man who can't stop adding to the repertory. He has recently embarked on making San Francisco-style French bread, bread sticks, even homemade potato chips. Under the circumstances I confess to still being startled when I come upon a pineapple upside-down cake, although perhaps I shouldn't be since this book is, after all, called American Boulangerie and many of the bakers are American. And when I, with my passion for Italian bread and *pasticceria*, do a double take at the grape focaccia with cream pored over the top, Pascal gives a little French shrug, smiles and says it's a French version, then smiles even more widely when he tells me that among the biggest hits at the bakery are meringues the size of baseball gloves. They are among the newest sweets and people can't get enough of them! Big, crunchy meringues walk out the door by the dozens. They may be made of egg whites but that doesn't mean that sweet butter and cream and yolks aren't used in prodigious quantities. French pride in the ingredients is clear from the sign, prominently displayed, that says in large letters, *"Tout ici est au beurre,"*—"Everything here is made with butter."

Even those of us who live nearby and walk to the bakery know that we'll have to be patient during the holidays. There are even more double-parked cars then and the line stretches up

the block and sometimes around the corner. I remember a couple of years ago when I realized I was a couple of desserts short for a large Thanksgiving dinner. I rushed to get in line with everyone else. I happened to meet a friend and we were talking as we moved slowly along when she suddenly looked at her watch and gasped. She was late and had to leave immediately to pick up her daughter, but before departing she made me promise to hold her place until she came back. Half an hour later there she was and there I was, still not having quite made it into the interior of the bakery. Everyone remembered and welcomed her back as we edged our way forward. That's what it's like at our neighborhood Boulangerie where an air of celebration and camaraderie is so often in the air.

It is exciting to see how important Boulangerie Bay Bread has become to the neighborhood in such a short time. The warmth, the good smells, the delicious tastes, the atmosphere in which pleasure and friendship blend easily have made it a favorite meeting place. Those buttery croissants! Those incomparable walnut baguettes! Those fig and prosciutto sandwiches! Those fruit tarts! How did we ever live without them?

THE BOULANGER'S APPRENTICE

ONE MORNING, NOT VERY LONG AGO, I was eating breakfast with my family. We were sitting around the kitchen table in our apartment, which is above our bakery on Pine Street, in San Francisco. Like most days, I had taken a basket downstairs and pulled an assortment of freshly baked breakfast pastries off the racks. My wife, Virginie, and I were talking, and Oscar, the baby, was eating and playing with a spoon. But my two daughters, Juliette and Pauline, were just sitting there, staring at the pastries. I asked them, "What's wrong?" and they both looked up at me and said, "Nous voulons du pain,"—"we want some bread."

As I walked back downstairs to get them a baguette to chew on, I smiled and shook my head, thinking about how much my daughters reminded me of myself at their age. Of course, like all kids, I liked to eat desserts and pastries. But for as long as I can remember, what I loved even more was fresh bread. I just had this thing about it—the flavor, the smell, the texture. I can't tell you why. It wasn't as if I came from a long line of bakers. I was just fixated on bread. And not only bread. I was crazy about the bakery, too.

Every day, my mom would send me down to Monsieur Audouin's boulangerie in our little village—Paillet, near Bordeaux—to pick up a couple of baguettes. I would inhale that smell of fermenting yeast and flour, breathe in that moist air, and peer past the counter into the bake-house, where M. Audouin, who also happened to be the town's mayor, would be working away. And for some reason I felt right at home.

I can't quite remember exactly how those trips to the baker turned into an apprenticeship. It happened without any discussion or planning. It wasn't something anyone told me to do, or something I had to do for money. It just happened, and then it gathered its own momentum, like dough rising in a warm place.

With my parents, Micheline and Jean Rigo, 1962.

By age 5, I was already "all business".

It started when I was seven years old. I would show up at the bakery every Saturday afternoon and hang around for an hour or two, watching everything and talking with "the guys." The bakers didn't seem to mind having me around. I didn't get in the way, but I don't think I was much help at first. I guess you could say I was more like a mascot.

After a while, though, M. Audouin figured out that I might actually be able to take some work off his hands, and I got my first real assignment, helping with the *galette des rois.* At Boulangerie Audouin, this cake, which is usually made only at Christmastime (there's a recipe for it on page 131) was a year-round specialty, and my official entrée into the business was filling the puff pastry with frangipane cream. Eventually, I was allowed to cut the pastry rounds myself and assemble the *galettes* on baker's trays. After I had mastered that, I learned how to put the trays in the oven with a peel—juggling and turning all the trays without disturbing the *galettes'* perfect round shape—and how to judge the exact moment when they were perfectly baked.

In France, you have the *boulanger*—the bread baker, who usually makes some pastries. And then you have the *pâtissier*—the pastry chef who runs a shop filled with elegant confections. That kind of shop, the *pâtisserie*, is really more of an urban thing. There can be a lot of showmanship and attitude involved. Out in the country, where I grew up, the boulangerie usually does it all—bread, pastries, cakes, cookies, tarts, and all kinds of little treats. Maybe that's what keeps them a little more real and grounded. *Pâtissiers*—at least in those days—could be a bit of a pain in the neck. *Boulangers* have always been the fun ones. And my buddies at the bakery were no exception.

I would look forward to Saturdays all week long. Sometimes I'd even show up after school, just to stand around, breathe in the air, and eavesdrop. In a small French village, every bit of gossip eventually filters through the boulangerie, and I quietly took it all in. Then there were the bakers' stories of their exploits with women. For a long time, I had absolutely no idea what they meant, but it felt very grown-up just being allowed to listen. After a while, it all started to

make sense, and my imagination would run wild filling in the missing details. Now, looking back, I realize that I learned everything there was to know about life in that steamy room—years before I had actually experienced any of it.

By the time I was eleven, I had been allowed to cut my first loaf of bread. That's a big moment—the moment when you take the blade in your hand and hold the dough with your fingertips, and you learn how to deftly cut just the right amount for a loaf. I still love that feeling of the dough against my fingertips and the blade teasing it apart, and I still do it just for the pure pleasure of the process.

I still love that feeling of the dough against my fingertips and the blade teasing it apart, and I still do it just for the pure pleasure of the process.

By then I had absolutely no doubt that I was going to become a professional baker. That is, if my other dream of being a professional soccer player didn't work out. So I kept both options open and spent every spare minute when I wasn't in school either kicking a soccer ball around or working at the bakery.

In my mid-teens, M. Audouin sold his bakery, and I got a job in the next town over, Lestiac, at the boulangerie of M. Bernard Contraire. Well, I shouldn't really say "job," because I was paid in bread, croissants, and an occasional kick in the butt. But M. Contraire was understanding about letting me go to my soccer matches, and by then, I was actually earning plenty of pocket money playing in local leagues.

Working for M. Contraire turned out to be a real stroke of luck—and a real education— because he was a Compagnon du Tour de France-a member of a select artisanal bakers' guild.

Plus ça change… The village boulangerie in Paillet, where my life as a baker began, still makes all of my childhood favorites.

The apprenticeship for becoming a *compagnon*—the "tour de France" itself—is a process that involves several years of living and working all over the country. It's an ancient, highly respected tradition. The *compagnons* still proudly wear their special gold earring as a symbol of their status, and they are regarded as the elite of their trade. By working for M. Contraire, I was able to do my tour de France without ever leaving home, because he had experienced everything there was to know about French baking—from the Parisian style to the specialties of Alsace, Brittany, Provence, and everywhere in between.

I kept working and kept playing soccer all through high school and five years of university. Eventually, based on what I had learned on the job, I was able to pass the exam for the *certificat d'aptitude professionelle*, the official certification without which no one can open a real bakery in France. But I still wasn't ready to open my own place. I went to Paris—because in France, when you're serious about a profession, sooner or later, that's just what you do—and worked at a couple of famous boulangerie/pâtisseries.

Eventually, I decided it was time to make a go of bread baking—but not in France. By the late '80s in France, the writing was on the wall. Bakers—like all tradespeople there, were faced with really tough economic and political limitations, and I thought I'd test my wings in a place with more opportunities to work hard and succeed: the United States.

I had been to Los Angeles on vacation and it seemed like a good place to start. In the course of doing various odd jobs and trying to sell wine to restaurants for a friend in France, I met Michel Richard, an extraordinary pastry chef—well, a brilliant chef in general, and a fantastic person. Michel was just about to open a new restaurant in L.A., The Broadway Deli, which featured a wood-fired oven. He was delighted to find out that I was a lifelong *boulanger*, and before I knew it, he had offered me a job developing the restaurant's bread recipes.

Everybody loved that bread. And when I told Michel I wanted to start a wholesale bakery, he said he would be a customer, and so would all his friends in the business. So I took the plunge, bought an old French oven from a bakery in Mexico, rented a warehouse and started a wholesale business called "Bread Only." Apparently, L.A. was ready for good bread. Within six months I was selling to the top seventy restaurants and hotels in the city. I was also working twenty-hour days and sleeping in my van or on top of the flour sacks, but I didn't mind, because I'd done all that before—and I knew that coming to America had been the right move. I was on my way.

After a few years, I was really missing Europe, so I decided to go for the next best thing: San Francisco—and the Napa Valley, which feels a lot like Bordeaux. After a year spent opening and developing Panorama Baking with a San Francisco-based restaurant group, I bought the Giusto bakery and ventured out on my own again. That's when Bay Bread was born.

As a baker, you are always very aware of the quality and cost of your raw materials, especially the flour. So, when the opportunity arose to purchase our own flour mill, I jumped at the chance. The mill in question, Central Milling Company, in Logan, Utah, is more than 150 years old. It's the largest producer of organic flour in the west, and until 25 years ago, it was still completely water powered. I am proud to say that, to this day, it provides all of the flour we use. I believe the quality and flavor of that traditionally milled organic flour have had a lot to do with our success.

In January of 1999, I took over an old Victorian building that was once a French laundry on Pine Street, and turned it into a bakery. When it came time to put something on the sign board outside, I just had them put the word "Boulangerie." I really didn't think that little bakery would be much of a retail store. I was only planning to bake bread there and mostly sell it wholesale, and the storefront was basically the packing room for that wholesale business. But we thought we might as well put some bread in the window to sell to customers off the street.

Within a few days, you couldn't find a parking space on the whole block. Word spreads quickly in San Francisco, especially when the word is "food." People had begun to line up for bread outside our shop all morning long. So, I thought I would make some croissants just for fun. The first day I made them, they sold out in twenty minutes. The next day we made more— and we made almond and chocolate ones, too. A few days later, we thought, "Why not try some miniature *palmier* cookies?" We put them in little bags and before we knew it we were selling 200 bags a day. Then the San Francisco Examiner gave us a great review, and that was it. No turning back.

Bit by bit, we kept adding new breads and pastries, and people seem to love them. Today, we have more than seventy items in the bakery. Along with the classic bread and pastry items, there are special things for every season and every big holiday, along with regional specialties from all over France—the kind of things I learned to make during my stay-at-home "tour de France" back in Lestiac. And all of that is what you will find in this book.

I think what these recipes have in common—and what has made our bakery unique—can be expressed in a single word that defines everything we do: authenticity. I don't just mean that we make exact copies of the breads and pastries you would find in a boulangerie in France. I am talking about a respect for tradition that comes through as soon as you walk into the shop; you can see it, smell it, hear it, and of course, taste it, and I wouldn't want to have it any other way.

The techniques and tools, the rolling pins, the resting times, even the words we use to describe the baking process—all of this comes from a long, rich history. To work in this way takes down-to-earth, straightforward people who love what they do absolutely and with all their soul; patient, clear-headed people who put tradition and quality ahead of ego and shortcuts. I'm lucky to be surrounded by people like that every day.

These days, I think we are all more hungry than ever for simple, honest authenticity, in every part of our lives, and it feels good to share that kind of approach through our bakery, and now through this book. For the most part, it is not meant to be a book of trendy inventions, easy solutions, or instant gratification. Instead I hope it will give you guidelines to learn from—a sort of mini-apprenticeship in the craft of the *boulanger.*

We have tried to capture the methods and recipes for making our baked goods as clearly and accurately as possible. But if you really want to connect with tradition and experience authenticity, you do have to do some work. No book can teach you everything. If you want to learn to transform flour and water into something fantastic and sustaining, there is only one way. Like a baker's apprentice, you do it over and over and over again, and every time you mix that flour and water, you learn, with your hands and your eyes and your palate, something new and fascinating.

If you want to learn to transform flour and water into something fantastic and sustaining, there is only one way...you do it over and over and over again ...

So here I am, living above the bakery with Virginie, Juliette, Pauline, and Oscar. Our days begin with bread and pastry, and our lives are filled with the aroma of the bakery—the powerful, comforting, smells of yeast and steam. My kids breathe in those smells. They see the importance of hard work, the value of respect for the customer, and most of all, the beautiful results that simplicity and authenticity can bring. Those are the gifts I want most to give to them, and I hope this book will give you a taste of them, too.

Looking back at my life so far, it occurs to me that what I have really done is to end up right where I began. I have tried to re-create for my family, myself, and everybody around us all the things I loved most about my own childhood. And that is what I will keep trying to do. Because, like a great round loaf of country bread, the *boulanger's* apprenticeship has no beginning and no end. It is a circle, and if you are very lucky, it lasts your whole life long.

INGREDIENTS AND TOOLS OF THE BAKER'S TRADE

Baker's Notes

Great baking is equal parts technique and ingredients. The technique part can take a lot of time and patience to master. But these days, really good ingredients are getting easier to find all the time. At the Boulangerie, we take a lot of pride in working with the best raw materials we can get our hands on, and we used them to test the recipes in this book. We've assembled these basic notes to familiarize you with the kinds of ingredients that we feel make a noticeable difference in the taste, texture, appearance, and appeal of the finished product. Start with the best and you're already halfway there.

Flour

We recommend using organic flours if they're available. Health food stores and many supermarkets carry a variety of organic flours, and they're also available through several mail-order companies (see "Resources," page 174).

Different types of flour contain varying amounts of gluten, the protein that is activated when flour is moistened and mixed. Flours with a high gluten content are referred to as "hard," while flours with low gluten content are called "soft"—a distinction you can feel if you rub different flours between your fingers.

Harder flours are used in bread recipes, as they have more elasticity for rising. Softer flours are used when a tender, crumbly texture is desired, as is the case with cakes and cookies. The wheat flours used in this book, from hardest to softest in order, are high-gluten, bread, all-purpose, and pastry. In recipes calling for pastry flour, cake flour can be substituted. Other flours, however, are not interchangeable in the recipes and should not be freely substituted. The proteins in buckwheat and rye flour do not form gluten, so when these flours are used, wheat flour is generally added to keep the finished product from being dense and heavy.

TAPIOCA FLOUR—a starch used as a thickening agent. Unlike cornstarch, tapioca flour doesn't break down when frozen.

CORNSTARCH—a fine, white powder derived from the endosperm of the corn kernel. It is used as a thickening agent and widely available in grocery stores.

CORNMEAL—coarsely ground dried corn widely available in grocery stores. Yellow cornmeal is used in the Peach Cornmeal Upside-Down Cake.

Salt

Sea salt is preferred in all our recipes for its intense, clean flavor.

Leavenings

BAKING SODA—a chemical agent used to leaven baked goods containing acidic ingredients. It can also be used to help neutralize the tangy flavor of those ingredients. When baking soda, an alkali, is combined with the acid in a recipe (such as the acids in buttermilk, chocolate, or honey), a chemical reaction occurs, releasing carbon dioxide, which causes the batter or dough to expand. Because this reaction occurs immediately upon contact, batters and doughs containing baking soda as their sole leavening agent usually need to be baked right away.

BAKING POWDER—a combination of baking soda, an acid or acid-reacting salt, with a starch added to prevent lumping due to moisture absorption. Most baking powder is double-acting, meaning that it releases a small amount of carbon dioxide upon contact with moisture, but the majority of the gas is released in the presence of heat. Once its ingredients are mixed, a recipe made with double-acting baking powder can sit for some time before baking without the leavening losing its power. Both baking soda and baking powder should be stored in a cool, dry place and should be replaced every four months to ensure their efficacy.

YEAST—can be fresh or dry. We use compressed yeast which is highly perishable and should be stored in the refrigerator. You can find it at many specialty foods stores and gourmet grocery stores in the refrigerated section. If compressed yeast is unavailable, active dry yeast—the kind sold in small packets in the baking section of grocery stores—can be substituted using the following ratios: 1 package active dry yeast = 1/4 ounce active dry yeast = 2 1/4 teaspoons = .6 ounce compressed fresh yeast. A basic equation for calculating the amount of active dry yeast to substitute is to use 40 percent of the amount of compressed yeast specified, and dissolve the dry yeast in four times its weight of warm (110°F) water. For example, if a recipe calls for 1 ounce of compressed yeast, you can substitute 3/8 ounce of dry yeast dissolved in 1 1/2 ounces of warm water. Yeast causes leavening by converting the sugars in a dough into carbon dioxide and alcohol. The carbon dioxide is trapped in the dough, causing it to rise.

The alcohol formed by yeast adds flavor to the bread or pastry. Yeast is a living organism and is sensitive to heat, cold, and salt. Temperatures higher than 140°F will kill yeast, while temperatures below 80°F will inhibit its leavening ability. Salt can also reduce yeast's ability to leaven and is therefore often added

later in a recipe with the majority of the flour, thus giving the yeast a head start.

Sweeteners

Besides adding sweetness, sugar gives baked goods a nice brown color, it is a nutrient for yeast and it makes doughs more tender. Following are the kinds of sugar we use at the Boulangerie.

GRANULATED SUGAR—the most commonly used of all sugars and sweeteners. When a recipe in this book calls for sugar, use granulated sugar. It is derived from either sugarcane (the kind we prefer) or sugar beets.

BROWN SUGAR—white sugar to which molasses has been added; it is available in both light and dark forms. When recipes in this book call for brown sugar, always measure it by packing it firmly into the measuring cup.

POWDERED SUGAR—also known as confectioners sugar is finely ground granulated sugar with a small amount of starch added to prevent clumping.

COARSE OR PEARL SUGAR—also known as decorating sugar, is available at specialty foods and cake decorating stores. It is bright white with large irregular chunks that don't dissolve when sprinkled on top of baked goods. It adds an attractive appearance and a nice crunch.

CORN SYRUP—made from cornstarch that has been treated with enzymes to convert it to more simple compounds. It is available in both light and dark forms, the dark versions containing added caramel color and flavoring.

HONEY—adds moisture and delicate flavor to many baked goods and gives a soft chewy texture to cakes and cookies. At the bakery we use a light amber honey, but any good-quality honey will do. Experiment with different varieties to find the ones you like best in baking.

Dairy Products

BUTTER—always use unsalted butter, as the amount of salt in salted butter varies, and that difference can affect the flavor and consistency of our recipes. We use Plugra, a European-style butter that has less water and more butterfat than traditional American butter—qualities that are particularly important in *viennoiserie*. Plugra is a brand name, a contraction of *plus gras*, French for "more fat." European-style butters are generally made with cultured milk. They lend a richer, more intensely buttery-nutty flavor to recipes and can be purchased at many specialty food stores and gourmet supermarkets. Several companies in this country have begun to offer butter made in this style. Always wrap butter when storing it in the refrigerator, as it absorbs flavors rapidly. If you won't be using it soon, wrap it well and freeze it for up to 3 months.

EGGS—we use extra-large eggs, and we don't recommend using eggs of other sizes, which could affect volume, flavor, and baking times. Always buy eggs that are as fresh as possible and store them in their carton in the refrigerator. The fresher the egg, the more volume you'll have when whipping the white. Letting eggs come to room temperature before using them also will increase their whipped volume, so take them out of the refrigerator an hour or two before you need them. When whipping egg whites, it's important that your mixing bowl and utensils be spotlessly clean and free of any grease or fat, such as butter, oil, cream, or egg yolk. Egg yolk (or other proteins) mixed with the whites will inhibit their ability to trap air and increase in volume. When separating eggs, if some yolk falls in with the whites, use the eggshell to scoop it out. The yolk is attracted to the shell and can be fairly easily and effectively removed from the whites in this way.

MILK—we use whole milk, which contains at least 3.5 percent butterfat. Using lowfat or skim milk in a recipe instead of whole milk will change the texture and flavor of the finished product and is not recommended.

CREAM—manufacturing cream or heavy cream with a milk fat content of at least 36 percent is preferred in all recipes calling for heavy cream.

SOUR CREAM—adds acidity, moisture, and richness to recipes. It must contain at least 18 percent butterfat. In recipes calling for sour cream, crème fraîche may be substituted.

CRÈME FRAÎCHE—fermented, thickened cream that can be purchased at many grocery stores. It is also very easy—and inexpensive—to make your own: In a glass container, combine 1 cup heavy whipping cream with 1 tablespoon buttermilk and let the mixture stand, covered, at room temperature for forty-eight hours to thicken. Crème fraîche will keep in the refrigerator for up to two weeks. For the recipes in this book, we do not recommend substituting sour cream for crème fraîche.

Fruits and Vegetables

At the Boulangerie we prefer to use fresh, seasonal, locally grown produce, organically grown if it is available. Of course, most supermarkets now carry fruits and vegetables that are traditionally seasonal—like raspberries and asparagus—year-round, although they tend to be much more expensive and probably not organic if purchased out of season. One alternative to paying high prices for fresh fruit out of season is to replace the item with its dried equivalent. The amount needed for a given recipe will vary, as dried fruit usually needs to be soaked in water (or liquor) in order to soften and plump it. It lends a different—often more intense—flavor to a recipe than its fresh counterpart. Another alternative is to substitute high-quality frozen or canned fruit. Look for those packed with little or no added sugar.

Oil

SUNFLOWER OIL—preferred in any recipe that calls for oil because it is light and neutral-tasting.

OLIVE OIL—a light mild-flavored, cold-pressed olive oil is best for our recipes as opposed to a full-bodied, fruity extra virgin olive oil.

Nuts

Almonds, hazelnuts and walnuts are the nuts most often used in baking. Like all nuts, they have a high oil content and should be properly stored, or they will become rancid and unusable. Store nuts in airtight containers in a cool, dark place or in the freezer. Almonds are available in a variety of forms, including whole, sliced, or slivered; and can be purchased natural (skin on) or blanched (skin off). Almonds are also used to make almond paste, available for special pastry items. Hazelnuts, also known as filberts, are available both natural and blanched.

The flavor of all nuts is enhanced by toasting. To toast nuts, preheat the oven to 350°F and spread the nuts on a baking pan in a single layer. Toast them for about 10 minutes or until they just begin to brown. Cool completely before chopping.

To chop nuts coarsely, chop by hand on a cutting board. Nuts can also be chopped in a food processor fitted with a steel blade, by pulsing the motor on and off. Watch carefully to avoid over-processing, which will turn the nuts into a butter or paste.

To make a nut meal or flour, as in the recipes for *Financier* or Parisian Macaroons, grind blanched, sliced nuts in a food processor, pulsing until you have a very finely ground meal with the consistency of cornmeal. Flour or sugar added to the nuts while grinding often helps prevent the nuts from turning into butter or paste. Nut meals are often available at specialty foods stores or markets.

Chocolate

CHOCOLATE—as with most ingredients, the highest-quality chocolates are generally the most expensive. While very high-quality chocolates, such as Valrhona and Scharffen Berger, are great for baking, slightly less expensive alternatives, such as Callebaut and Cacao Barry, will also provide delicious results. Avoid inferior chocolates containing artificial flavors and fats other than cocoa butter, which negatively affect how they melt and the flavor they impart.

Bittersweet chocolate is not to be confused with unsweetened chocolate, it contains less sugar than semisweet chocolate and therefore has a more intense chocolate flavor. *Gianduja* is a blend of hazelnuts and milk chocolate.

In recipes calling for cocoa powder, use unsweetened Dutch-process cocoa (often simply called "Dutch Cocoa"). This process uses an alkali to neutralize acid and evenly disperse the cocoa butter, resulting in a dark, rich cocoa powder.

Chocolate scorches easily. The safest way to melt it is in a bowl set over a pot of gently simmering water, stirring often to prevent burning. Be sure that no steam or water gets into the bowl, as this will cause the chocolate to seize and become a grainy, unmeltable mass. If the chocolate does seize, it can sometimes be salvaged by adding 1 teaspoon of vegetable oil per ounce of chocolate. Chocolate can also be melted in the microwave: Place it in a microwave-safe container and microwave it for 30 seconds on high power, then stir and repeat the process until the chocolate is melted. Chocolate should be stored in an airtight container in a cool, dark place.

Extracts

VANILLA, ALMOND, AND LEMON—pure, natural extracts will provide a truer and more concentrated flavor than an artificial or imitation flavoring. Extracts stored in a cool, dark place will keep indefinitely; exposing them to heat and light will cause them to lose potency.

ROSE WATER—made from fragrant rose petals, is distilled using the same processes as that used for making liqueurs. It is very concentrated, so use it sparingly. You'll find it in Middle Eastern markets.

Liqueurs and Spirits

RUM—we prefer to use dark rum—such as Myers or Bacardi Select—which imparts more characteristic rum flavor to recipes than light rum.

CALVADOS—a brandy distilled from apple cider, which comes from the Normandy region of France. If Calvados is unavailable, you can substitute applejack or brandy.

GRAND MARNIER—an orange-flavored liqueur from France is widely available and widely used in cooking. Cointreau may be substituted.

Miscellaneous

COCONUT—unsweetened or desiccated coconut is dried, unsweetened coconut that has been ground to the consistency of coarse cornmeal. You can find it in Asian markets.

BLACK CHERRY—preserves are available in most specialty foods stores. If you have access to a good Italian market, ask for the preserved sour cherries known as amarena.

GELATIN—sheets are an excellent jelling agent. The sheets generally weigh $1/10$ ounce and are available in specialty foods stores. They must be softened in cold water before they can be dissolved. After softening, squeeze out the excess liquid and add to the recipe as indicated. Unless so labeled, gelatin is not acceptable for Kosher eating. (See sidebar page 108.)

BEESWAX—is a must for making *cannelés*. You can find it in many health food stores, as well as some specialty foods stores. Make sure it is labeled "Pure."

Tools of the Trade

There are thousands of pieces of equipment available to home bakers today. Here are the ones we use most often at the bakery.

ELECTRIC MIXER—a free-standing electric mixer is a great investment if you're a frequent baker. It will likely come with three invaluable attachments: the dough hook, the paddle, and the whisk. If you bake a lot, a second bowl is invaluable.

MEASURING CUPS—come in two forms, dry and liquid. Dry measuring cups should have sturdy handles and straight sides. They are often sold in sets of $\frac{1}{4}$-, $\frac{1}{3}$-, $\frac{1}{2}$-, and 1-cup measures. When measuring dry ingredients such as flours and sugars, the cup is dipped into the ingredient and then leveled off using the back of a knife or spatula. Liquid measuring cups have a pouring spout, and the increments are clearly marked on the side. Measuring spoons are used for both dry and liquid ingredients.

NONSTICK BAKING MATS—also known as French baking mats, are silicone-coated, flexible fiber mats. They are ideal for baking cookies, as they are reusable, easy to clean, and safe to use with food.

OFFSET SPATULA—sometimes called an offset palette knife, is a wooden- or plastic-handled spatula with a dull stainless-steel blade with a rounded end. The length of the blade ranges from 4 to 14 inches. The most practical size for baking is a $1\frac{1}{2}$-inch wide blade that is 8- to 10-inches long. The term "offset" refers to the fact that the blade is bent at almost a 90° angle a few inches below the handle and then bent again to become parallel to the handle. This design allows you to spread and level icing or batter without touching it with your hand. It's ideal for leveling genoise batter in the baking sheet and spreading fillings on top of doughs.

OVEN THERMOMETER—is indispensable for ensuring that your oven is properly regulated.

PANS—before you begin baking, check any recipe for the size and type of pan you will need. Following are the pans we use most frequently at the bakery. Many of these are now available made of silicone.

BAKING SHEETS—professional-quality baking sheets are made of heavyweight aluminum and have a rolled edge. Their sides are 1-inch high and they measure about 12 by 18 inches. They are ideal for making genoise as well as baking cookies. Professional baking sheets perform better and last longer than traditional "cookie sheets."

BÛCHE DE NOËL MOLDS—are made of tinned steel, and have a half-round shape. They are 20-inches long by 3-inches wide and 2-inches high. They have a capacity of about 8 cups.

CAKE PANS—are made of heavy-duty aluminum and have 2-to 3-inch high, straight, seamless sides.

CHEESECAKE PANS—are made of heavy-duty, seamless aluminum. They have 2- to 3-inch high, straight, seamless sides and a removable bottom plate for easy unmolding.

FRIAND MOLDS—are small rectangular nonstick molds used for *financiers*. They are 4-inches long by 2-inches wide. The sides of the molds are sloped at a 45° angle.

LOAF PANS—the best loaf pans are made of aluminized steel and are available in a variety of sizes.

MADELEINE PLAQUES—are made of either tinned or nonstick steel. The indentations for the madeleines should be about 3-inches long by $1\frac{3}{4}$-inches wide. Each plaque will generally make 12 madeleines.

SPRINGFORM PANS—are made of tinned steel, with a removable side wall; a clamp tightens the side wall against the bottom of the pan.

TART PANS—are most commonly round pans with fluted edges and a removable bottom to release tarts easily. They are made of tinned steel and available in a wide range of diameters, heights, and shapes. Check your recipe for appropriate size before beginning.

PARCHMENT PAPER—also known as baking paper, is a specially treated nonstick paper. Available in roll or sheet form, it is widely used to line baking sheets and pans to keep food from sticking. It often eliminates the need for buttering and flouring the pan. When baking cookies, parchment paper can be used a second time by flipping it over.

PASTRY BAGS— are cone-shaped bags made of either plastic, nylon, or cloth that are available in a variety of sizes. When fitted with a metal or plastic piping tip (also called a pastry tip), a pastry bag is used to pipe out batters, icings, whipped cream, and doughs. It is very important to wash pastry bags thoroughly in warm, soapy water after each use. Always remove the piping tip before washing. After washing, rinse well and dry the bag inside and out, then allow to air-dry completely before putting away. The most frequently used piping tips are plain, producing a smooth edge, or star-shaped, producing a fluted pattern.

PASTRY BRUSHES—are small, flat brushes ranging in width from ½- to 3-inches wide. They should be made of natural bristles, which retain their softness and pliability better than nylon or other synthetic bristles. Pastry brushes are used to apply egg wash, melted butter, and glazes. They're also handy for brushing off excess flour from doughs. Wash pastry brushes thoroughly after each liquid use and air-dry before putting away.

PASTRY CUTTERS—also known as cookie cutters, are available in numerous shapes and graduated sizes as well as with plain and fluted edges. If you invest in sturdy, high-quality cutters and store them properly, they'll last you a lifetime.

RUBBER SPATULAS—are also called bowl scrapers. They are used most for scraping down the sides of bowls while mixing. Buy yourself a few sturdy, heat-resistant ones, especially if you're planning to try recipes that involve stirring hot liquids, like our Flan recipe.

ZESTER—a hand tool used to cut the paper-thin zest of citrus fruit—the part in which the essential oils are concentrated, while leaving the bitter white pith behind. It is usually about the size of a paring knife and has 5 small holes along the top edge of its blade. In recent years, razor-sharp rasps, available at specialty stores, have become the preferred choice for zesting among professional chefs and bakers.

LES PAINS
Bread

In France, the idea of "daily bread" is not taken lightly. A trip to the boulangerie for a fresh loaf is, for many people, still a daily—if not twice-daily—ritual. In a densely populated area of Paris, a neighborhood boulangerie would be likely to sell around 3,000 baguettes a day. San Francisco is a little different. Our American Boulangerie Bay Bread, started with bread, but quickly came to feature many other traditional French baked goods. Bread remains the cornerstone of our business in terms of volume, but not in terms of variety. Rather than making many types, we've chosen to focus on a few classic ones—the most popular of which are *pain au levain*, *baguettes*, *pain de mie*, and *fougasse*—with a selection of variations based on them. The recipes for these breads are astonishingly simple, at least as far as their ingredients go. Essentially, they are made from flour, water, yeast, and salt. There are two keys to making them. First, use the best ingredients you can find— ingredients like local organic grapes for the *levain* starter and freshly milled organic flours. Second, practice. Don't try making these breads for the first time when you have company coming over. Give yourself a few rehearsals. Experiment, adjust, and make mental notes as you go. You'll be surprised what flour, water, and yeast can teach you. Patience, flexibility, persistence, and pleasure in simple things—those are the lessons of daily bread.

LEVAIN NATURE

Natural Bread Starter

At Boulangerie Bay Bread, most of the bread includes a bit of this natural-yeast starter made from fermented grapes, both for leavening and for its distinctive, tangy flavor. We've been using the same mother starter at all of our bakeries and restaurants for several years now, taking a pinch of it in a plastic tub to whatever new location we're opening as our own "christening" ritual. There's a lot of mystique surrounding natural starters, but they're really not particularly hard to make and not as fragile as you might imagine. Think of a homemade starter as a low-maintenance house pet—a living thing to be treated with respect and a lot of common sense. This one gets its start when wild, airborne yeast feed on the sugar in the grapes, causing fermentation. If the starter gets too warm, the yeast will die; too cool and the starter will be less lively and active. Feed it when it is hungry and show it some love, and it will reward you with great bread and plenty of entertainment for years.

8 ounces organic grapes

1 cup organic bread flour

5 cups (1¹/₂ pounds) organic
all-purpose flour

1¹/₂ cups water

MAKES ABOUT 2¹/₂ POUNDS STARTER

1. To make the *levain* starter: In a medium bowl, crush the grapes with the back of a large spoon. Cover with plastic wrap and let sit at room temperature, until fermented, 2 to 3 days. (Fermentation has taken place when the surface appears foamy and there is a slight yeasty smell. Even if the juice has not fermented after 3 days, continue as if it has. It will just take a bit longer to rise in the next step, as there is less wild yeast in the mixture.) Strain the grapes and their juice through a fine-mesh strainer; reserve the juice and discard the grapes. You should have ½ cup of juice; if not, add enough water to measure ½ cup.

2. In a medium bowl, combine the juice and bread flour and mix until a soft, sticky dough forms. Turn it out onto a lightly floured work surface and knead until smooth, 2 or 3 minutes. Place the young *levain* into a large, lightly floured bowl, cover with plastic wrap, and let proof until doubled in size, 6 to 8 hours. (If your juice was not actually fermented to start, this can take up to 24 to 36 hours. The young levain should have bubbles and look very much alive.)

3. Add the all-purpose flour and water to the *levain* and mix thoroughly. Turn it out onto a lightly floured work surface and knead until smooth, 2 or 3 minutes. Return the dough to the lightly floured bowl, cover with plastic wrap, and let rise again, until doubled in size, 6 to 12 hours. At this point, your starter is ready to use. If you will not be using the starter immediately, punch it down, form it into a nice, smooth ball, and return the dough to the bowl. It can then be stored, covered, and refrigerated, for up to 24 hours. Bring the starter to room temperature before proceeding with your chosen recipe.

4. Feeding for long-term conservation: If you will not be using your starter within 24 hours, it may be stored up to 1 week in the refrigerator, tightly covered in plastic wrap, without attention. After 1 week has passed, you will need to feed the starter to keep the yeast alive. This is different from "refreshing" your starter for making bread the next day. To feed the starter, weigh the original starter. You will be adding one-fourth of its weight in flour and one-eighth of its weight in water. For example, if you have 1 pound of starter, you will add 4 ounces flour and 2 ounces water. Mix well and knead into a smooth ball. Cover and let it remain at room temperature for 2 hours. Date your starter to remind you when to feed it again and return it to the refrigerator until the night before you will be making bread.

5. Refreshing the starter: The night before you will be making a recipe requiring some of the starter, you will need to refresh it. This refreshment must be done even if you have fed your starter recently.

In step 4 you are adding flour and water to keep it alive for up to 1 week. And you are not leaving it out at room temperature for more than 2 hours. The starter must be refreshed the night before baking for it to have just the right amount of strength and liveliness for our recipes. First you must decide how much starter you will need for the next day, including an additional amount to reserve for the next time. Assuming you want 1 pound of refreshed starter, add one-fourth of its weight in flour, or 4 ounces, and one-eighth of its weight in water, or 2 ounces. Mix it well and leave at room temperature at least 6 hours. You can now measure and remove the portion needed for the recipe. Cover and refrigerate any remaining starter and remember to date it and "feed" it again in 1 week! Once you have a starter going, you will be using some and feeding or refreshing it at various intervals depending on your bread-baking needs. Use just enough of the older starter to feed or refresh it according to the instructions and discard the rest.

PAIN AU LEVAIN NATURE
Country Bread with Natural Fermentation

Once you've mastered levain starter, all you need is good flour, water, and salt to enjoy wonderful homemade country-style bread with a mildly tangy bite, a crisp, substantial crust, and a light but toothsome interior. This makes a single giant loaf or two smaller ones. Following the recipe, you'll find three great variations, all of which are popular at our Boulangerie. The Walnut Bread is excellent with good cheese or butter and thinly sliced prosciutto. For an unusual treat, do what the vintners in Bordeaux do during the harvest: Rub a slice of day-old walnut bread with garlic and eat it with grapes—and wash it all down with a glass of red Bordeaux. The Pecan-Raisin Bread is nice for breakfast, toasted, with butter, honey, or a little maple syrup. And the Cranberry-Pumpkin Seed version is just right for a Thanksgiving menu—not too sweet and fantastic with gravy.

1. In a large bowl, combine the starter, flour, water, and salt. Mix thoroughly until the dough comes together. Turn it out onto a clean work surface and knead it until smooth, 8 to 9 minutes. Form it into a round ball and place the dough into a very large floured bowl, cover with plastic wrap, and let rise, 3 to 6 hours. The longer it rises and ferments, the more sour the final taste of the bread will be; however, you will get less volume.

2. Again, turn the dough out onto a clean work surface. If you don't want to bake the dough as a single loaf, divide it into 2 equal portions at this point. Shape each dough portion as follows: Push down on the dough and fold it in on itself to bring the edges into the middle and form it into a rough ball. Flip it over onto an unfloured work surface. (The unfloured surface will help create tension when forming the dough into a ball.) Place your hands, with fingers spread out, over the top of the dough. (Pinkie fingers and edges of your palms should be resting on the work surface on either side of the ball.) Using a gentle downward pressure, rotate the dough, in quick, tight circles (your pinkies will be tucking in the bottom of the ball) to form a tight, smooth ball. This is your final shaping, so make it nice. Place the single large loaf or the 2 smaller loaves on a lightly floured baking sheet. Let rise 1 to 3 hours, until the dough feels springy and a dimple left by your fingertip in the dough fills back in rather quickly. If in doubt, err on the side of less time; never overproof the dough.

$1/2$ **pound Natural Bread Starter (page 20), at room temperature**

$6^1/2$ **to 8 cups organic bread flour**

3 cups water, at room temperature

2 tablespoons ($1^1/2$ ounces) sea salt

MAKES ONE ROUND 4-POUND LOAF, OR TWO ROUND 2-POUND LOAVES, OR FOUR 1-POUND LOAVES

3. One hour before baking, place a roasting pan on the bottom of a gas oven, or on the lowest rack directly above the heating element if electric, and preheat the oven to 425°. Sprinkle a little bit of flour on the top of the loaf and, using a single-edge razor blade, quickly slash the bread by making a cross-cut on top. Place the loaf in the oven, quickly but carefully pour 1 cup water into the hot roasting pan, and close the door as quickly as you can to trap the steam. (It's the steam that will help the bread to achieve its full volume and beautiful color.) After 3 minutes, pour another 1 cup water into the hot roasting pan, opening and closing the oven door as quickly as possible. Continue baking the bread for 50 to 60 minutes or until deeply browned. If you think the bread is not baked enough but has enough color, finish baking it with the oven door slightly ajar, until the base of the bread sounds hollow when tapped. Let cool completely on a wire rack before slicing.

You may use the following variations to create four different breads from the same batch of Pain au Levain Nature dough, dividing it into 1-pound portions, and kneading in the specified ingredients.

Walnut Bread: In step 1, at the end of mixing, divide the dough into 1-pound portions. For each portion of dough you want to flavor, knead in 3 ounces (1 cup) coarsely chopped, lightly toasted, room-temperature walnuts. The more you knead it, the more color the dough will take on from the walnuts. Proceed to shape, rise, and bake the loaves as directed in steps 2 and 3.

Pecan-Raisin Bread: In step 1, at the end of mixing, divide the dough into 1-pound portions. For each portion of dough you want to flavor, knead in 2 ounces (³⁄₄ cup) coarsely chopped, lightly toasted pecans and 2 ounces (¹⁄₃ cup) golden raisins. Proceed to shape, rise, and bake the loaves as directed in steps 2 and 3.

Cranberry-Pumpkin Seed Bread: In step 1, at the end of mixing, divide the dough into 1-pound portions. For each portion of dough you want to flavor, knead in 2 ounces (¹⁄₂ cup) toasted pumpkin seeds and 2 ounces (¹⁄₃ cup) dried cranberries. Proceed to shape, rise, and bake the loaves as directed in steps 2 and 3.

PAIN COMPLET
Whole Wheat Bread

A heartier, nuttier-tasting version of our classic Pain au Levain Nature *(page 23). The variation made with chestnut flour has an appealing smoky flavor that pairs well with fromage blanc, cream cheese, or goat cheese. I love it toasted for breakfast with a little honey on top. The rye variation is really good with oysters and salted butter, smoked fish, or blue cheese.*

½ pound Natural Bread Starter (page 20), at room temperature

6½ to 8 cups organic whole wheat flour

3 cups water, at room temperature

2 tablespoons (1½ ounces) sea salt

MAKES ONE ROUND 4-POUND LOAF, OR TWO ROUND 2-POUND LOAVES

1. To make the bread: In a large bowl, combine the starter, flour, water, and salt. Mix thoroughly until the dough comes together. Turn it out onto a clean work surface and knead it until smooth, 8 to 9 minutes. Form it into a round ball and place the loaf into a very large floured bowl, cover with plastic wrap, and let rise, 3 to 6 hours. The longer it rises and ferments, the more sour the final taste of the bread will be; however, you will also get less volume.

2. Again, turn the dough out onto a clean work surface. If you don't want to bake the dough as a single loaf, divide it into 2 equal portions at this point. Shape each of the portions as follows: Push down on the dough and fold it in on itself to bring the edges into the middle and form it into a rough ball. Flip it over onto an unfloured work surface. (The unfloured surface will help create tension when forming the dough into a ball.) Place your hands, with fingers spread out, over the top of the dough. (Pinkie fingers and edges of your palms should be resting on the work surface on either side of the ball.) Using a gentle downward pressure, rotate the dough, in quick, tight circles (your pinkies will be tucking in the bottom of the ball) to form a tight, smooth ball. This is your final shaping, so make it nice. Place the single large loaf or two smaller loaves on a lightly floured baking sheet. Let rise 1 to 3 hours, until the dough feels springy and a dimple left by your fingertip in the dough fills back in rather quickly. If in doubt, err on the side of less time; never over-proof the dough.

3. One hour before baking, place a roasting pan on the bottom of a gas oven, or on the lowest rack directly above the heating element if electric, and preheat the oven to 425°. Sprinkle a little bit of flour on the top of the loaf and, using a single-edge razor blade, quickly slash the bread by making a cross-cut on top. Place the loaf in the oven, quickly but carefully pour 1 cup water into the hot roasting pan, and close the door as quickly as you can to trap the steam. After 3 minutes, pour another 1 cup water into the hot roasting pan, opening and closing the oven door as quickly as possible. Continue baking the bread for 50 to 60 minutes, or until deeply browned. If you think the bread is not baked enough, but has enough color, finish baking it with the oven door slightly ajar until the base of the bread sounds hollow when tapped. Let cool completely, on a wire rack, before slicing.

Chestnut Flour Bread: In step 1, at the end of mixing, divide the dough into 4 equal portions. For each portion of dough you want to flavor, mix in ½ cup plus 1½ tablespoons chestnut flour, 3 tablespoons water, and an extra pinch of salt. Proceed to shape, rise, and bake the loaves as directed in steps 2 and 3.

Rye Flour Bread: In step 1, at the end of mixing, divide the dough into 4 equal portions. For each portion of dough you want to flavor, mix in 1 cup plus 3 tablespoons rye flour, 6 tablespoons water, and an extra pinch of salt. Proceed to shape, rise, and bake the loaves as directed in steps 2 and 3.

PAIN COMPLET AU MIEL
Honey Whole Wheat Bread

When we wanted to offer our customers a healthy toasting bread for breakfast and sandwiches, we developed this recipe, adding honey and baking it in loaf pans so it can be cut into uniform slices.

1. In the 5-quart bowl of an electric mixer, whisk together the water, honey, and yeast until the yeast is dissolved. Add the whole wheat flour, bread flour, salt, and sunflower seeds. Using your hands, mix together just until a loose dough is formed and most of the flour is moistened. Fit the mixer with a dough hook and mix on low speed until a uniform ball is formed, 2 to 3 minutes. Increase speed to medium-high and mix an additional 8 minutes, until smooth and elastic. Turn the dough out onto a lightly floured work surface and knead briefly to form a smooth ball. Let the dough rest, covered with plastic wrap, on the work surface or in a large bowl, for 30 minutes.

2. Wipe two 9 x 5 x 3-inch loaf pans with the vegetable oil. Set aside. Divide the dough into 6 equal portions. Form each portion into a rough ball by pushing down on the dough and folding it in on itself to bring the edges into the middle. Flip the balls over onto an unfloured work surface. (The unfloured surface will help create tension when forming the dough into balls.) Working with 1 ball of dough at a time, place your hands, with fingers spread out, over the top of the dough. (Pinkie fingers and edges of your palms should be resting on the work surface on either side of the ball.) Using a gentle downward pressure, rotate the dough, in quick, tight circles (your pinkies will be tucking in the bottom of the ball) to form a tight, smooth ball. Repeat with the remaining dough. Place 3 balls of dough in a line in each loaf pan. The dough will rise above the top of the pan, so do not lay a cloth directly on top of the pans. Let rise in a warm, draft-free place, 1 to 1½ hours, until the dough feels springy and a dimple left by your fingertip in the dough fills back in rather quickly. Do not overproof. While the bread is rising, center a rack in the oven and preheat the oven to 375°.

3. Lightly brush or mist the top of the loaves with water and immediately place the loaves in the preheated oven. Bake for 40 minutes or until a nice mahogany brown. Remove the loaves from the pans and place them, right side up, directly onto the middle rack of the oven. Continue baking, with the oven door slightly ajar, an additional 10 to 15 minutes, until dry and crusty. Let cool completely, on a wire rack, before slicing.

3½ cups water, at room temperature

¾ cup honey

⅝ ounce (3¾ teaspoons) compressed fresh yeast

4 cups organic whole wheat flour

4 cups organic high-gluten, unbleached bread flour

5 teaspoons salt

2⅜ ounces (½ cup) sunflower seeds

Vegetable oil, for pans

MAKES TWO LOAVES

PAIN DE MIE

White Sandwich Bread

This classic French white bread has a firm texture and a nice delicate crumb. It's just the thing for making Croque Monsieur (page 69), kids' sandwiches, or French toast. You can also trim the crust and use it to make little triangular finger sandwiches.

¹/₃ cup water, at room temperature

¹/₃ ounce (2 teaspoons) compressed fresh yeast

¹/₂ cup milk

4 ounces (¹/₂ cup) European-style butter, softened, plus additional for pans

2¹/₃ cups organic bread flour

1 tablespoon sugar

2 teaspoons sea salt

1 large egg, beaten, for egg wash

MAKES ONE LOAF

1. In the bowl of an electric mixer, whisk together the water and yeast. Let rest until the yeast is creamy, about 5 minutes. Place the bowl on the mixer and fit with the dough hook. Add the milk, 4 ounces butter, bread flour, sugar, and salt. Mix on low speed, turning the machine on and off a few times, until it seems the flour will stay in the bowl and not fly about. Increase the speed to medium and mix, stopping to scrape down the sides and bottom of the bowl as needed, until the dough is smooth and elastic, about 10 minutes. Transfer the dough to a large, floured bowl. Cover with plastic wrap, and let rise, at room temperature, until doubled in size, about 2 hours.

2. Butter a 9 x 5 x 3-inch loaf pan and set aside. Punch down the dough and turn it out onto a lightly floured work surface. Shape the dough into a rectangle with a 9-inch width. Start rolling the dough from the short edge. Roll tightly, pressing down on the seam with the heel of your hand as you roll. Transfer the dough roll to the prepared pan, seam side down. (The bread may look small in the pan, but don't worry—it will grow.) Cover tightly with plastic wrap and let rise until the dough is level with the top of the pan, about 2 hours. While the bread is rising, center a rack in the oven and preheat the oven to 375°.

3. Brush the top of the loaf with egg wash. Bake for 40 minutes or until dark brown. Remove the loaf from the pan and check for doneness. It should sound hollow when tapped on the bottom. If you have any doubts, put the loaf back in the oven (without the pan) and leaving the door slightly ajar, bake for 5 more minutes. Transfer to a wire rack to cool completely. Store in a plastic bag and slice as needed. It will stay fresh for at least 5 days. The bread can also be frozen, wrapped airtight, for up to a month.

FOUGASSE SUR PLAQUE
Yeasted Flat Bread

Fougasse is the focaccia of southern France—a rich, white flour dough pressed into a sheet pan before baking. Our version uses a bit of levain *starter to make it extra fluffy and tasty, but if you don't have any starter on hand, you can omit it and still make a great* fougasse. *It's good as a snack or table bread and an ideal choice for making pressed or grilled* panini. *Baked pizza-style with a savory topping (below) it can be a satisfying light meal. We've also provided our sweet variation—the popular grape-studded* Tarte Sucrée.

1. In the bowl of an electric mixer, whisk together ¼ cup of the water and yeast. Let rest until the yeast is creamy, about 5 minutes. Place the bowl on the mixer and fit with the dough hook. Add the remaining 1½ cups plus 2 tablespoons water, starter, butter, 3 tablespoons oil, flour, sugar, and salt. Mix on low speed, turning the machine on and off a few times, until it seems that the flour will stay in the bowl and not fly about. Increase the speed to medium and mix, stopping to scrape down the sides and bottom of the bowl as needed, until the dough is soft and slightly elastic, and cleans the sides of the bowl, about 10 minutes. Transfer the dough to a large, floured bowl. Cover with plastic wrap, and let rise, at room temperature, until doubled in size, about 2 hours.

2. Preheat the oven to 375° and line a 12 x 18 x 1-inch baking sheet with parchment paper. Set aside. Fold the dough over on itself to deflate it, and turn it out onto a lightly floured surface. Press and stretch the dough into a rough rectangle. Transfer to the prepared baking sheet and, using your hands, pull and stretch the dough until it is the size of the baking sheet. Using your fingertips, dimple the entire surface of the dough. Generously brush with olive oil, and then let rise, uncovered, at room temperature until doubled in height, about 2 hours. Once again, dimple the surface of the dough with your fingertips, and brush with more olive oil. Bake for 20 to 25 minutes or until golden brown. Transfer to a wire rack and cool slightly, about 5 minutes. (Once cooled, extra *fougasse* can be wrapped airtight and frozen for up to a month. Thaw, still wrapped, at room temperature, and then warm in a 350° oven before serving.)

Tomato, Zucchini, and Parmesan Fougasse: While the shaped dough is rising, thinly slice two zucchini and two ripe tomatoes. Season with salt, pepper, and chopped fresh herbs. Brush the proofed dough with olive oil; drain the zucchini and tomato slices of any excess liquid and arrange nicely over the dough. Sprinkle with grated Parmesan cheese and bake as directed.

Grape-Cream Tarte Sucrée: Push about ½ pound ripe seedless grapes into the dough, and drizzle 3 tablespoons heavy cream over the top. Sprinkle with 2 tablespoons sugar and bake as directed.

1¾ cups plus 2 tablespoons water, at room temperature

¾ ounce (1½ tablespoons) compressed fresh yeast

¼ Natural Bread Starter (optional; page 20), at room temperature

3 ounces (6 tablespoons) European-style butter, softened

3 tablespoons olive oil, plus additional for brushing the top

5¼ cups organic white flour

4½ teaspoons sugar

4½ teaspoons sea salt

MAKES ONE 12 x 18-INCH RECTANGULAR BREAD

COURONNES DE "CHEZ NOUS"
Chez Nous Crowns

When we opened our Mediterranean restaurant, Chez Nous, around the corner from our Boulangerie Bay Bread, we wanted to serve a signature bread in the same playful spirit as the lively "small plate" items that make up the menu. After a little experimentation, we came up with these miniature bread crowns, which were an immediate hit and remain a big part of the success of the place. They're easy to make and fun to eat, and I encourage you to try your own flavoring variations, using the ideas that follow as a starting point. You can also simply shape these as miniature baguettes, making the traditional diagonal slashes across the top just before baking.

1^1/$_4$ cups water, at room temperature

1 ounce (2 tablespoons) compressed fresh yeast

3 cups (16 ounces) organic white flour

2 teaspoons sea salt

MAKES TWO CROWNS

1. In a large bowl, whisk together the water and yeast. Let rest until the yeast is creamy, about 5 minutes. Add the flour and salt all at once and mix until well combined. Turn it out onto a lightly floured work surface and knead by hand until smooth, 6 to 8 minutes. Cover with a clean tea towel and let the dough rise, on the lightly floured work surface, until doubled in size, about 1½ hours.

2. Divide the dough in half and form each portion into a thin roll, about 12 inches long. Transfer to a lightly floured baking sheet and let rest until relaxed, about 10 minutes. Form each roll into a horseshoe shape without actually bringing the two ends together at the bottom. Using kitchen scissors, make two cuts along each outside edge of each horseshoe (see photo). Cut only one-half to three-quarters of the way into the dough. Cover with a clean tea towel and let the crowns rise until doubled in size, about 35 minutes.

3. Place a roasting pan directly on the bottom of the oven. Preheat the oven to 350°. Place the crowns on the baking sheet in the oven, quickly but carefully pour 1 cup water into the hot roasting pan, and close the door as quickly as you can to trap the steam. Bake until golden brown, 20 to 25 minutes. They are better if slightly underbaked rather than overbaked. Transfer to a wire rack and let cool slightly. Serve warm.

Curry-Raisin Couronnes: In step 1, after you have added the flour and salt, but before you have kneaded the dough, mix in 1 ounce curry powder and 2 ounces (¼ cup) raisins. Continue to knead, let rise, and bake as directed.

Walnut-Scallion Couronnes: In step 1, after you have added the flour and salt, but before you have kneaded the dough, mix in 1 ounce (¼ cup) chopped, toasted walnuts and 1 ounce (¼ cup) chopped scallions. Continue to knead, let rise, and bake as directed.

Pumpkin Seed Couronnes: In step 1, after you have added the flour and salt, but before you have kneaded the dough, mix in 2 ounces (½ cup) pumpkin seeds. Continue to knead, let rise, and bake as directed.

Poppy-Sesame Seed Couronnes: In step 1, after you have added the flour and salt, but before you have kneaded the dough, mix in ½ ounce (2 tablespoons) poppy seeds and ½ ounce (2 tablespoons) sesame seeds. Continue to knead, let rise, and bake as directed. (Sprinkle a few more poppy and sesame seeds on top.)

LES VIENNOISERIES
Croissants and Pastries

The simplest way to tell you what the baker's term *viennoiserie* means would be to say, "croissant, puff pastry, and brioche." From these three kinds of dough, you can make pretty much all of the classic pastries of the French breakfast table. The first two involve the time-consuming technique of layering butter into the dough. Brioche, on the other hand, is a buttery yeasted egg bread. You find *viennoiserie* in both *pâtisseries* and boulangeries all over France. Because croissant and puff pastry require lots of space, time, and refrigeration, they're generally a bit more refined and tasty when made by a *pâtisserie*, which is better set up for that kind of thing. To really do it right takes a lot of practice and experimentation. I got my hands-on training at the boulangerie where I apprenticed—making I don't know how many thousands of little buttery things over the years I was there. You develop an instinct for how it should look and feel at every stage, and that's both the requirement and the reward for making it consistently great. The best tip I can give you, whether you are making puff pastry or croissants, (besides "be patient!") is this: You want the dough and the butter to be as close in texture to each other as possible. It should feel like you are layering together two things that are already intimately related. How you get that is a question of time and temperature. It takes some playing around, but that's the fun of *viennoiserie*.

PÂTE FEUILLETÉE

Puff Pastry

The whole key to puff pastry is to work fast and keep things cold. Stay focused on the job, and try not to forget where you are in the process—it's really important to keep turning and folding in the right direction to make it evenly layered. After the final rolling, when you're all ready to cut the dough into whatever shape you need, you're actually not ready. You need to put the dough back in the refrigerator one last time so it relaxes. Otherwise, it will shrink when you bake it and what went into the oven looking promisingly beautiful will come out misshapen and unattractive. Also, any time you trim the dough, use a very sharp knife and make quick, deft cuts. If the blade is blunt, it will mash the layers together and the edges won't rise as nicely.

4¼ cups high-gluten flour or bread flour

¼ cup sugar

2½ teaspoons salt

1 cup plus 2 teaspoons water

3 ounces (6 tablespoons) unsalted butter, melted

14 ounces (1¾ cups) unsalted butter, at cool room temperature

MAKES ABOUT THREE POUNDS DOUGH

1. In the bowl of an electric mixer fitted with the paddle attachment, beat the flour, sugar, salt, water, and melted butter on medium speed until well mixed, about 1 minute. Work quickly and do not overwork the dough. Transfer the dough to a large piece of plastic wrap, form it into a rough rectangle, enclose the dough in the plastic wrap, and refrigerate for 1 hour. Meanwhile, put the remaining 14 ounces butter between 2 pieces of plastic wrap and beat it with a rolling pin, turning as necessary, until softened. The butter should be malleable but not too soft. Set aside in a cool place—the butter will later be spread on the dough as you start the folding process.

2. Place the refrigerated dough on a well-floured work surface and dust the top of the dough lightly with flour. Using a rolling pin, push down on the dough to start flattening it, and then roll it into a 20 x 10-inch rectangle, ¼-inch thick, with the long sides running from left to right. (It might feel that you're rolling sideways, and well, you are.) Carefully brush off any excess flour from the dough. Starting on the right side, and leaving a 1-inch border, slap and spread on the butter, using your fingers, over two-thirds of the rectangle. Fold the dough into thirds: starting with the left side, fold at the butter line as if closing a book, and then fold the right side up and over the top layer. You should end up with a stack of 3 thick layers of dough, each separated from the next by a layer of butter.

3. As you prepare to make the first turn of the dough, keep in mind the importance of rolling the butter evenly along the length and width of the rectangle as you roll the dough. Adjust the pressure on the rolling pin as necessary, rolling harder or more evenly, to achieve a smooth, even, dough-enclosed butter sandwich. To begin your first turn, turn the dough 90 degrees on your work surface so the closed fold is at the top and, rolling lengthwise, roll it into a 20 x 10-inch rectangle. Brush off any excess flour and fold into thirds as above, starting with the left side and ending with the right. At this point, you have finished one turn. Rotate the dough 90 degrees so the closed fold is at the top, and repeat the rolling and folding process. The second turn is complete. After the second turn, or any time the dough is too soft to work with, transfer to a parchment paper–lined baking sheet and refrigerate, covered in plastic wrap, for about 30 minutes, or until the dough is chilled and relaxed. Each time the dough is refrigerated, make an indentation in the dough with your fingertip for each turn completed. Repeat this rolling and folding process, rolling out the dough lengthwise every time, four more times for a total of six turns. After the sixth turn, let the dough rest a good hour in the refrigerator.

4. Store the dough, as is, well wrapped in plastic wrap. The dough can be kept refrigerated up to 3 days, or frozen up to 10 days. If frozen, thaw the dough, still wrapped in plastic, in the refrigerator before using.

Folding puff pastrie with sugar makes these great Petits Palmiers: recipe follows.

PETITS PALMIERS
Little Palm Leaves

These crispy little cookies were among the first products we sold at Boulangerie Bay Bread, packed in little plastic bags. Today, we sell 10,000 of them every week. To me, palmiers should be one size-only: small. The big ones are harder to make and have to be turned during baking so they brown evenly. The little kind don't need flipping, and they cook quickly and caramelize beautifully all over. And, more importantly, they're just the right size to pop into your mouth.

1¹/₂ **pounds** (¹/₂ **recipe) chilled Puff Pastry Dough (page 38)**

1¹/₄ **cups sugar**

MAKES SIXTY TO SIXTY-FIVE COOKIES

1. Place the refrigerated dough on a work surface that has been sprinkled with ¼ cup of the sugar. Sprinkle an additional ¼ cup of the sugar evenly over the dough. Roll the dough lengthwise until very thin, about ⅛ inch thick. Sprinkle both the work surface and the top of the dough with the remaining ¾ cup sugar. Using a very sharp knife, trim the edges of the dough to form a 36 x 8-inch rectangle, then cut the rectangle into thirds. (At this point, you should have 3, 12 x 8-inch pieces.) Working with just 1 of the 3 rectangles at a time, turn the dough so the 12-inch side runs lengthwise from left to right. Fold both the left and the right sides in toward the middle, to meet but not overlap. Then, fold both the right and left sides in toward the middle again, to meet but not overlap. Finally, fold just the right side completely over the left. If you look at the end of the roll, it will look a bit like a heart. If you count the layers, you will find 8 (4 in each half of the heart). Wrap in plastic wrap and refrigerate 30 minutes.

2. Meanwhile, preheat the oven to 400°. Line a baking sheet with parchment paper. Using a sharp knife, cut the refrigerated roll crosswise into ⅜-inch-wide slices. Place the slices 2 inches apart, cut-side down, on the prepared baking sheet, and bake for 12 minutes or until the sugar caramelizes and turns golden brown and crispy. Transfer to a wire rack and let cool. The *palmiers* can be stored in an airtight container up to 1 week.

CHAUSSONS AUX POMMES

Apple Turnovers

The essential balancing act for making perfect apple turnovers like these is to get as much filling as possible inside without compromising the structure of the pastry. If you overfill, the fruit will seep out the edge and burn. Underfilling means not enough flavor. When they're just right, you get a bit of apple in every bite. If you want to make an even simpler turnover, you can do it with uncooked apples the way my mom did when I was a kid. For each turnover, she would slice half a medium-sized apple paper thin, sprinkle it with sugar, top it with a little crème fraîche, and then seal it up. She also did the same thing with apricots or with cherries, tossed in a bit of rice flour to absorb their liquid. I remember how fantastic her simplest chausson of all tasted: the filling was nothing more than a big spoonful of lemon curd.

1. Peel, core, and cut the apples into small dice. In a medium saucepan, combine the apples and honey and cook over medium heat until tender, about 8 minutes. Transfer half of the mixture to a medium bowl and, using a potato masher, mash into a thick purée. Stir in the remaining apples and let cool completely.

2. Preheat the oven to 375°. Remove the puff pastry from the refrigerator and place on a lightly floured work surface. Using a rolling pin, roll into a 10 x 20-inch rectangle, ⅛-inch thick. Using a round cutter, 5 inches in diameter, cut out 8 dough circles. Spoon about ¼ cup of the applesauce on the bottom half of each circle, leaving a ½-inch border around the bottom edge of the semicircle. Brush the bottom edge with egg wash and close each turnover by folding the top half of dough over the filling and pressing the edges together. Using the tip of a small knife, gently cut five slits across the top of each *chausson*. Brush the tops with the egg wash and bake on a parchment paper-lined baking sheet for 20 to 25 minutes or until golden brown. Transfer to a wire rack to cool slightly. Serve warm or at room temperature.

2 pounds Granny Smith apples

2 tablespoons honey

³/₄ pound (¹/₄ recipe) chilled Puff Pastry Dough (page 38)

1 egg, lightly beaten, for egg wash

MAKES EIGHT TURNOVERS

CROISSANTS AU BEURRE FIN
Croissants

You are about to embark on an adventure. Let me share a few tips. First, follow the rules: Croissant dough is equal parts science and art, and the science part can't be glossed over. Second, never overproof croissant dough—your finished product will be spongy, not flaky. Third, although you might be used to seeing big croissants in bakeries these days, my advice is to keep them small; bigger generally means chewier, and the perfect croissant is flaky and a little crunchy. Fourth, do a double egg-wash, once before the final proofing and once just before baking. This will give your croissants a really professional-looking, satiny finish and a deep, mahogany color. Finally, let croissants cool slightly before you eat them, or the steam will make them too soft. Master all of that, and you will have more than a mere piece of pastry. You will have—to quote the San Francisco Examiner's *poetic review of our croissants—"that first kiss from a new love."*

1. In the bowl of an electric mixer fitted with the dough hook, combine the yeast, milk, water, flour, sugar, and salt and mix on low speed until a soft dough forms on the hook, 1 to 2 minutes. Scrape down the sides and bottom of the bowl as needed. Increase the speed to high and work the dough until it is smooth and elastic, about 2 minutes. Do not overwork the dough or the final product will not be as flaky. Transfer the dough to a floured baking sheet, cover with plastic wrap, and refrigerate for 8 to 12 hours.

2. When you are ready to work with the dough, place the butter between two pieces of plastic wrap and beat it with a rolling pin, turning as necessary, until softened. The butter will later be spread on the dough; it should be malleable but not too soft. Set aside in a cool place.

3. Place the refrigerated dough on a generously floured, large work surface. Dust the top of the dough with flour, and then roll the dough into a large 12 x 6-inch rectangle, $^3/_{16}$-inch thick, with the long sides running from left to right. (A large, heavy, ball-bearing pin makes quick work of rolling. The heavy weight of the pin makes it much easier to roll out buttery, elastic doughs quickly.) Roll mostly lengthwise, but occasionally switch to rolling widthwise to help keep the edges and corners as square and even as possible. Carefully brush off any excess flour from the dough. Starting on the right side, and leaving a 1-inch border, slap and spread on the butter, using your fingers, over two-thirds of the rectangle. Fold the dough into thirds—starting with the left side, fold at the butter line as if closing a book, and then fold the right side up and over the top layer. You should end up with a stack of 3 thick layers of dough, each separated from the next by a layer of butter.

$^1/_2$ **ounce (1 tablespoon) compressed fresh yeast**

$^3/_4$ **cup whole milk**

$^1/_3$ **cup water**

$3^3/_4$ **cups high-gluten flour or bread flour**

$^1/_4$ **cup plus 1$^1/_2$ teaspoons sugar**

2 teaspoons sea salt

$^3/_4$ **pound (1$^1/_2$ cups) best-quality unsalted butter, at cool room temperature**

MAKES ABOUT TWENTY CROISSANTS (OR ABOUT 2$^1/_2$ POUNDS DOUGH)

4. To begin your first turn, turn the dough 90 degrees on your work surface so the closed fold is at the top and, rolling lengthwise, roll it into a 12 x 6-inch rectangle. Brush off any excess flour and again fold into thirds as described in step 3, starting with the left side and ending with the right. Pull on the dough as needed to make the corners square. At this point, you have finished one turn.

5. There are three more turns to make. Mark on the parchment that this is turn 1, cover the dough with plastic wrap and refrigerate for about 1 hour.

6. For the second and future turns, place the dough on your floured work surface so the closed fold is at the top, and then roll the dough lengthwise, as for the first turn. Remember to brush off excess flour before folding into thirds and to jot down what number turn it is before refrigerating. Do two turns at a time,

refrigerating for 20 to 30 minutes after each pair of turns. After the fourth and final turn, refrigerate the dough, covered in plastic wrap, for a good hour before shaping the croissants. (At this point, the dough may also be frozen, covered tightly in plastic wrap, up to 1 month. If frozen, thaw the dough, still wrapped in plastic, in the refrigerator before use.)

7. To cut the dough, place the refrigerated dough on a generously floured work surface with the closed fold of the dough at the top. Dust the dough with flour and roll lengthwise into a large 10 x 17-inch rectangle, ¼-inch thick. Cut the dough in half lengthwise, to form two 5 x 17-inch strips of dough. With the dough placed lengthwise in front of you, running from right to left, measure in 1½-inches from the right on the bottom edge of the dough and make a small nick with your knife. Make an angled cut, starting at the nick

on the bottom edge and ending at the right corner of the top edge. Discard this trimming. Next, make an angled cut, parallel to the first cut, every 3 inches. Repeat with the second strip of dough. You will have ten, 3 x 5-inch angled "rectangles." Discard the final trimming. Cut each "rectangle," on the diagonal, to form two triangles each.

8. To shape each croissant, set the triangle on a lightly floured work surface with the tip of the triangle pointing towards you. Hold onto the base of the triangle with your right hand and, using your left hand, pull the point towards you, stretching the dough until it's almost double its original length. With your right hand, starting from the base of the triangle furthest from you, roll the dough towards you until the point is underneath. Pull gently on both ends of the rolled croissant and transfer to a parchment-lined baking sheet, curving the ends of the croissant slightly. Leave space for them to double in size. Repeat with remaining dough triangles. Brush the croissants with egg wash and let rise slowly, at room temperature, until puffy and doubled in size, 2 to 3 hours.

9. Preheat the oven to 375° and place the oven rack in the center of the oven. Brush the croissants once again with egg wash and bake for 15 to 20 minutes or until they are golden brown. Cool on a wire rack. The croissants are best eaten the day they are made. They also can be frozen, if wrapped airtight in plastic wrap, up to 1 month. Thaw overnight, still wrapped, and reheat in a 350° oven for 5 to 8 minutes.

CROISSANTS AUX AMANDES
Almond Croissants

In America, you find a lot of almond croissants made by rolling the dough around almond paste. That's actually not the way it's done in France. There, a croissant aux amandes usually means a fully baked croissant, cut in half, moistened with rum or syrup, and filled with a creamy almond filling. I think French bakeries invented them as a way to use up day-old croissants. I know in the boulangerie where I was an apprentice, I would start every day by splitting yesterday's croissants in half, filling them with almond pastry cream, and then drizzling them with chocolate. We tried the same kind of idea in San Francisco at our Boulangerie Bay Bread, but added the extra step of giving the filled croissants a quick second baking in a hot oven, so the almonds get toasty, the pastry cream on top browns just a bit, and the whole thing comes together in a wonderfully intense way. Well, the demand for our creation quickly exceeded our supply of day-old croissants, so now we bake plenty of extra fresh ones, just to be turned into croissants aux amandes. By the way, you can also do this with brioche. In France, we call that version bostok.

1. To make the almond filling: In the bowl of an electric mixer fitted with the paddle attachment, cream the ground almonds, granulated sugar, and butter on high speed for 3 minutes, until the mixture is smooth and creamy, scraping down the sides and the bottom of the bowl as needed. Add the pastry cream, eggs, flour, and almond extract and mix on medium speed for 3 minutes, stopping once midway to scrape down the sides and the bottom of the bowl. The filling should be very light and fluffy.

2. Slice a croissant in half horizontally, and spread the bottom half with about 3½ tablespoons of the almond cream. Cover with the top half of the croissant. Spread the top surface of the croissant with another 3½ tablespoons of almond cream. Place the sliced almonds in a shallow dish. Invert the croissant, cream side down, into the sliced almonds, pressing gently to make sure the almonds adhere to the cream. Transfer, almond side up, to a parchment paper–lined baking sheet. Repeat process with remaining croissants. Bake in a 400° oven for 10 minutes, or until the almonds are brown and the croissant is crisp. The almond cream will be soft in the middle but cooked on top. Generously dust with powdered sugar and eat while still warm.

ALMOND FILLING

6 ounces (1½ cups) very finely ground blanched almonds

³/4 cup granulated sugar

4 ounces (8 tablespoons) unsalted butter, at room temperature

¹/2 cup cold Crème Pâtissière (page 115)

2 extra-large eggs, at room temperature

¹/2 cup plus 2 tablespoons all-purpose flour

1 teaspoon pure almond extract

10 baked Croissants (page 43)

4 ounces (1¹/4 cups) sliced natural almonds

Powdered sugar, for dusting

MAKES TEN ALMOND CROISSANTS

CHOCOLATINES

Chocolate Croissants

Most people call these chocolate croissants pain au chocolat, *but in the southwestern part of France, we call them* chocolatines. *They're made by rolling croissant dough around a* baton *(a long thin bar) of chocolate. The ones I remember eating as a kid were made with a single bittersweet* baton *in the center. I would eat all around that center part and save it for a final burst of chocolate intensity, always wishing there could be a little more. Maybe that's why I decided to make our* pain au chocolat *at the boulangerie with two* batons *instead of one.*

1. To cut the dough, place the refrigerated dough on a generously floured work surface with the closed fold of the dough at the top. Dust the dough with flour and roll, lengthwise, into a large 10 x 30-inch rectangle, ¼-inch thick. Cut the dough in half, lengthwise, to form two 5 x 30-inch strips of dough. With the dough placed lengthwise in front of you, cut into ten 3 x 5-inch rectangles. Repeat with the second strip of dough.

1. To shape the *chocolatines*, place a rectangle widthwise on a lightly floured work surface; one of the 3-inch edges should be closest to you. Center one of the pieces of the chocolate on the bottom third of the rectangle. Brush the surface of the dough with the egg wash and then roll the dough, beginning at the bottom edge, up and over the chocolate. Continue rolling, finishing with the seam side down, on the bottom of the *chocolatine*. Transfer to a parchment paper–lined baking sheet, leaving space for them to double in size. Press down with your fingers and gently flatten the log to form a rectangle about 1-inch thick. Repeat rolling and flattening with remaining rectangles. Brush the *chocolatines* with egg wash and let rise slowly, at room temperature, until puffy and doubled in size, 2 to 3 hours.

2. Preheat the oven to 375° and place the oven rack in the center of the oven. Brush the *chocolatines* once again with egg wash and bake for 15 to 20 minutes or until they are golden brown. Cool on a wire rack. The *chocolatines* are best eaten the day they are made. They also can be frozen, if wrapped airtight in plastic wrap, up to 1 month. Thaw overnight, still wrapped, and reheat in a 350° oven for 5 to 8 minutes.

2¹/2 pounds (1 recipe) chilled Croissant Dough (page 43)

12 to 13 ounces flat bittersweet chocolate bars, snapped into 25 pieces (about ¹/2 ounce each)

1 egg, lightly beaten, for egg wash

MAKES TWENTY TO TWENTY-FIVE CHOCOLATE CROISSANTS

BRIOCHE
Brioche

For me, brioche is all about texture. The secret of light, delicate, rich-tasting brioche is getting as high a ratio of butter and eggs to flour as you can. That makes the dough somewhat tricky to work with because it is so soft, but the more flour you add, the more your brioche will be like egg bread, and the less of that meltingly airy texture the brioche will have. The colder the dough is, the easier it will be to handle, so be sure to give it a good chill in the refrigerator before shaping it, and once you start, work quickly. If at first you don't succeed, don't lose heart. There are many professional bakers in France who cannot, and will not, make brioche because their hands are simply too warm. Fortunately, I'm not one of those hot-blooded people.

2 tablespoons milk

1/3 ounce (2 teaspoons) compressed fresh yeast

4 extra-large eggs

2 tablespoons sugar

1 teaspoon sea salt

2 cups bread flour

6 ounces (3/4 cup) best-quality unsalted butter, softened

1 large egg, beaten, for egg wash

MAKES ONE LOAF

1. In the bowl of an electric mixer, combine the milk and yeast and let rest until the yeast is creamy, about 5 minutes. Fit the mixer with the dough hook, add the eggs, sugar, salt, flour, and softened butter to the yeast mixture, and mix on low speed just until the ingredients start to come together, a minute or two. Increase the mixer speed to medium and beat for about 10 minutes, scraping down the sides and bottom of the bowl, as well as the dough hook, as needed. During this time, the dough will become smooth and wrap itself around the dough hook. The dough will be soft and a bit sticky, and will make a slapping sound as it hits the side of the bowl.

2. Place the dough in a large floured bowl, cover tightly with plastic wrap, and let rise at room temperature until doubled in size, about 2 hours. Deflate the dough by punching it down in the bowl. Cover the bowl tightly with the plastic wrap and refrigerate the dough for at least 4 hours or overnight. The dough is now ready to be shaped into a loaf or used in any recipe using brioche dough. To freeze the dough, deflate the chilled dough, wrap it airtight in plastic wrap, and freeze up to 1 month. Let thaw, wrapped, in the refrigerator overnight.

3. To bake as a loaf: Butter a 9 x 5-inch loaf pan. On a lightly floured surface, shape the dough into an 8 x 4-inch rectangle. Starting from a short edge, roll the dough tightly, pressing down on the seam as you roll. Place the dough roll in the pan, seam side down. (The bread may look small in the pan, but don't worry, it will grow.) Cover the pan tightly with plastic wrap and let the brioche rise until it is level with the top of the pan, about 2 hours.

4. Preheat the oven to 375°. Brush the top of the loaf with the egg wash, and bake for 30 to 35 minutes, or until dark brown. Let the brioche cool in the pan for 30 to 45 minutes. If you remove the brioche from the pan while it is still hot and steamy, this delicate bread will collapse. Remove brioche from the pan and let cool completely on a wire rack. Store in a plastic bag up to 2 days, or freeze up to 1 month.

Pictured: Brioche and Brioche Tarte Sucrée

BRIOCHE TARTE SUCRÉE

Sugared Brioche Tart

If you're making brioche dough, make extra. You can use it to turn out a quick, luxurious-tasting tart like this one, which we enjoy in France for breakfast or as a snack. The little indentations you poke with your finger (recruit the nearest child to do this part; they love it) help keep the tart flat, as it should be, and give the crème fraîche something to hold on to as it bakes. Fresh fruit on top transforms this into a first-rate dessert, especially in the summer. Fruit or no fruit, a Tarte Sucrée needs to be eaten right away, while the crème fraîche is still warm and bubbly and hasn't soaked into the crust.

³/₄ pound (¹/₂ recipe) chilled Brioche
    dough (page 50)

1 cup crème fraîche

¹/₃ cup sugar

1 egg, beaten, for egg wash

1 ounce (2 tablespoons) unsalted
    butter, softened

MAKES ONE 10-INCH TART

1. Line a baking sheet with parchment paper and set aside. Gently shape the dough into a ball and let relax for about 10 minutes. On a lightly floured surface, roll out the dough into a 10-inch-diameter circle. Transfer to the baking sheet and let rise until doubled in size, 1¹/₂ to 2 hours.

2. Preheat the oven to 375°. Press your fingertips into the dough to make deep dimples all over the surface. Spread the crème fraîche evenly over the dough, leaving about a 1-inch border around the edge free of crème, and then sprinkle the sugar over the crème fraîche. Brush the border with the egg wash, dot the top with dabs of butter, and bake for 15 to 20 minutes or until the dough is golden brown. Transfer to a cooling rack. Serve warm or at room temperature.

VARIATION

Arrange thin slices of fruit (pears, nectarines, or apples are all good choices) over the crème fraîche before you sprinkle with sugar. Brush the edge with egg wash, dot the top with butter, and bake as directed.

ESCARGOTS CHOCOLAT NOISETTES
Chocolate and Hazelnut Brioche "Snails"

This is something we invented one day for a celebration at a local farmers' market: brioche dough rolled up jelly-roll style with pastry cream and chocolate chips, cut into individual "snails," and topped with hazelnuts—sort of an upscale cinnamon roll, without the cinnamon. They loved them at the farmers' market, and we've been baking them ever since.

1. Make sure your brioche dough is very cold before you start. On a lightly floured work surface, roll the dough into a 22½ x 9-inch rectangle, ⅛-inch thick, with the long sides running from right to left. Spread the pastry cream over the dough, leaving a ½-inch border free of pastry cream along the 22½-inch bottom edge (this will provide a better seal when the dough is rolled). Sprinkle the chocolate over the pastry cream (you can substitute some raisins or use some of both). Brush the border with some of the egg wash and then, starting from the long edge at the top of the rectangle, roll the dough over the filling like a coil. Seal the long end at the bottom and stretch the tube a little bit between your fingers. Using a serrated knife, cut into fifteen 1½-inch slices, or little "snails." Place the snails cut side down on parchment paper–lined baking sheets, leaving enough space for them to double in size. Brush the tops with egg wash and let rise, uncovered, until doubled in size, about 2 hours.

2. Preheat the oven to 375°. Push 4 to 5 whole hazelnuts into the top of each snail and bake for 10 minutes or until golden brown. Let cool on a wire rack. Serve warm, dipped into hot chocolate.

1½ **pounds (1 recipe) chilled Brioche dough (page 50)**

1 **cup Crème Pâtissière (page 115)**

6 **ounces bittersweet chocolate, coarsely chopped (about 1 cup)**

1 **large egg, beaten, for egg wash**

32 **to 40 whole hazelnuts (about 2 ounces)**

MAKES FIFTEEN SNAILS

TARTE TROPEZIENNE
Brioche Tart from Saint Tropez

This fluffy confection—a big brioche puff filled with a combination of pastry cream and honeyed whipped cream—is a specialty of bakers in the South of France, especially around Saint Tropez, where its name comes from. That explains the use of honey, a favorite ingredient of Mediterranean bakers. This would be just right for quatre-heures, the four-o'clock snack that's a national mid-afternoon tradition in France.

1. To make the *Tropezienne:* Preheat the oven to 375° and line a baking sheet with parchment paper. Set aside. On a lightly floured surface, roll out the dough into a 10-inch-diameter circle. Transfer to the baking sheet and let it rise until the dough is about 1-inch high, about 45 minutes.

2. Brush the egg wash over the top of the dough and sprinkle with the pearl sugar. Bake for 14 minutes, or until the dough is golden brown. Let cool completely on a wire rack.

3. To make the filling: In the bowl of an electric mixer fitted with the whisk attachment, combine the cream and honey. Whip on high speed to stiff peaks. Place the cold pastry cream in a large bowl. Using a large rubber spatula, quickly stir one-quarter of the whipped cream into the pastry cream, to lighten it. Then fold the remaining whipped cream into the lightened pastry cream.

4. To assemble the *Tropezienne:* Using a serrated knife, slice the cooled *Tropezienne* in half horizontally. Spread the filling on the bottom layer, leaving a ½-inch border around the edges free of filling. Replace the top layer. (The pressure of the knife when cutting will push the filling out to the edges.)

5. To serve, using a serrated knife, cut the *Tropezienne* into 8 pieces, wiping the knife clean between each slice. Place the slices on serving plates and finish with a dusting of sifted powdered sugar over each.

TROPEZIENNE

¾ pound (½ recipe) chilled Brioche dough (page 50)

1 extra-large egg, well beaten

2 tablespoons pearl sugar or coarse sugar

FILLING

1½ cups heavy cream

3 tablespoons honey

1 cup cold Crème Pâtissière (page 115)

MAKES ONE 10-INCH CAKE

LES QUICHES, LES TARTINES, ET LES SANDWICHES

Savory Tarts and Sandwiches

I love my job. When I get hungry for a little snack, a light lunch, or a quick supper, I just walk into the Boulangerie, and there is always just the right, satisfying thing to nibble on. It might be a slice of savory tart, a piece of quiche, a simple sandwich on a baguette, or a little country-style open-faced sandwich—what the French call a *tartine*. That's the feeling I like people to experience when they come into the shop: a lot of choices among simple, intensely flavored, savory items. I think it's the way we all like to eat more and more these days—small bites of very flavorful food, sometimes quite rich, sometimes very light, but always satisfying because every flavor has been thoughtfully chosen and carefully put together. These sorts of preparations are what you will find in this chapter: simple savory items that are some of the most pleasing little bites in the world.

ABOUT QUICHES AND SAVORY TARTS

The quiches we make at the Boulangerie are fairly thin and flat, and they are more about the ingredients than the custard. That's the real French way: just enough custard to hold everything together—almost the reverse of how most people make quiches in the United States. Savory tarts are like the pizza of France. And, as with pizza, the crust is all-important. In France, that crust would usually be either pâte brisée or puff pastry. Master those two basic doughs, and you can experiment with all kinds of toppings. As you'll see in our recipes, crème fraîche makes a simple, flavorful filling base for savory tarts of all kinds.

ABOUT TARTINES

A *tartine* is an open-faced sandwich. In France, the *tartine* is more of a country thing—a few simple toppings on a slab of crusty bread—while the sandwich on baguette is the more typical urban alternative. When we opened our second bakery, Boulange de Polk, we decided to offer a variety of *tartines* and sandwiches that could be made with minimal kitchen equipment and would hold up well in a bakery. In this chapter, you'll find some of our most popular creations. *Tartines* make great picnic food; you can always add a second slice of bread to help them travel better. They're also nice as a first course, served with a little mound of greens tossed in vinaigrette. And they work really well as party food—just cut them into bite-sized pieces, or prepare them on rounds of toasted baguette.

ABOUT SANDWICHES

In France we use butter the way Americans use mayonnaise. It's pretty much a requirement for sandwich making. Even a cheese sandwich will have a bit of butter on it. If you want to know the joy of a true French sandwich, it's simple. Start with a real baguette that was baked today—preferably one you bought from a local bakery, and so crisp and fresh you couldn't resist tearing off a piece to eat before you even got home. Cut it into sandwich-sized pieces on a slight diagonal (yes, the angle is part of the experience). Split those pieces lengthwise and spread on some really good butter, and now all you need is one more superb ingredient—a slab of cheese, a few thin slices of ham or salami, a piece of country-style pâté. Lettuce is optional. Cornichons are nice on the side.

PÂTE BRISÉE
Pie Dough

This is a basic short-pastry dough for tarts, quiches, or pies that always turns out flaky and buttery. Make sure the butter is quite cold, so it doesn't melt when you work the dough with your hands.

1. Have ready one of the following, depending on your chosen filling recipe: one round 11-inch-diameter, fluted metal tart pan with removable bottom; or one rectangular 12 x 4-inch tart pan with removable bottom; or six round 4-inch-diameter tartlet pans with removable bottoms.

2. In the bowl of an electric mixer fitted with the paddle attachment, combine flour and salt. Add the cold butter and mix on low speed until mixture resembles fine breadcrumbs, about 1 minute. Add egg, cold water, and lemon juice and continue mixing just until large lumps form. Turn out onto a lightly floured work surface and, using your hands, gather the mixture together. Using the heel of your hand, knead the dough gently, just until it holds together, about 30 seconds. Shape dough into a disk, wrap in plastic wrap, and refrigerate for at least 1 hour or overnight.

3. On a lightly floured work surface, roll out the chilled *Pâte Brisée* until ⅛-inch thick. Carefully transfer the pastry to your chosen tart pan, or tartlet pans, and trim the excess pastry by running your rolling pin over the top edge of the pan. Using a fork, lightly prick the bottom of the tart shell. Cover with plastic wrap and refrigerate for at least 1 hour or up to 1 day before using.

2½ cups all-purpose flour

¾ teaspoon salt

5 ounces (10 tablespoons) cold unsalted butter, cut into ¼-inch cubes

1 egg, lightly beaten

¼ cup cold water

½ teaspoon fresh lemon juice

MAKES ONE 11-INCH TART SHELL

PIZZA DU BOULANGER

Tomato, Olive, and Anchovy Tart

This splashy Mediterranean-style savory tart can be made with either Pâte Brisée (page 59) or Pâte Feuilleté (page 38). You can play around with all kinds of additional toppings, including artichokes, ham, or slices of roasted red and yellow bell pepper. If you're making it for people who appreciate anchovies, arrange the fillets across the top of the tart in a beautiful criss-cross pattern. If not, hide them among the olives and tomatoes, and I'll bet no one will object.

TOMATO CONCASSÉ

1¹/₂ pounds plum tomatoes, cored and bottoms lightly scored with an X

1 tablespoon olive oil

1 small onion, finely chopped

1 to 2 cloves garlic, finely chopped

Pinch dried herbs de Provence

1 tablespoon tomato paste

Salt and freshly ground black pepper

1 chilled, unbaked, rectangular 12 x 4 -inch Pâte Brisée tart shell (page 59)

1 pound mixed small tomatoes, such as cherry, golden, and grape, halved

¹/₂ cup pitted kalamata olives, sliced

6 canned anchovies in olive oil, drained (optional)

1 tablespoon extra virgin olive oil

Shavings of Parmesan cheese, for garnish

MAKES ONE 12 x 4-INCH RECTANGULAR TART

1. To prepare the tomato *concassé:* Bring a large saucepan of water to a boil over high heat. Add the plum tomatoes and blanch 10 seconds. Immediately remove the tomatoes from the boiling water, drain, and plunge into a bowl of ice water to stop the cooking. Gently peel the skins off the tomatoes. The skins should come off easily; if they don't, return them to the boiling water for another 5 to 8 seconds. Cut tomatoes in half, scoop out their seeds and discard, and chop coarsely. Set aside. In a large sauté pan, heat oil over medium heat. Add the onion and cook until soft, about 5 minutes, stirring occasionally. Stir in the garlic and cook until fragrant, about 1 minute. Add the chopped tomatoes, herbs de Provence, and tomato paste and season with salt and pepper. Cook uncovered, stirring often, until mixture is thick, 25 to 30 minutes. Let cool to room temperature.

2. Preheat oven to 425°. Place the chilled tart shell on a parchment paper–lined baking sheet. Spread the tomato *concassé* evenly over bottom of the tart shell. Arrange the tomato slices over the *concassé,* and top with the olives and then the anchovies. Drizzle the extra virgin olive oil over the top of the tart. Bake until the crust is golden and tomatoes have caramelized in places, about 30 minutes. Let cool in the pan, on a wire rack. Serve warm or at room temperature, garnished with shavings of Parmesan cheese.

QUICHE LORRAINE
Prosciutto, Ham, and Gruyère Quiche

Unlike typical versions of Quiche Lorraine, ours does not use bacon. I like it better with a combination of prosciutto and ham, which cuts down on some of the fat and gives the whole thing a more delicate flavor. If you want to play around with this recipe, just remember to use plenty of ham and cheese (or whatever ingredients you choose), and err on the side of less custard, rather than more. When I was growing up, this was the sort of dish we would serve as a main course for dinner and the leftovers as a first course for lunch or an afternoon snack the next day.

1. Preheat oven to 425°. Place the chilled tart shell on a parchment paper–lined baking sheet. Scatter the prosciutto, ham, and cheese evenly over the bottom of the tart shell. In a small bowl, whisk together the milk, crème fraîche, eggs, salt, and pepper. Pour milk mixture over the meat and cheese. Bake immediately until just set and the surface is golden brown, 40 to 45 minutes. Let cool in the pan, on a wire rack, for 10 minutes before serving. The quiche can be served warm or at room temperature.

1 chilled, unbaked, 11-inch Pâte Brisée tart shell (page 59)

5 ounces diced prosciutto (about 1 cup)

5 ounces diced ham (about 1 cup)

5 ounces shredded Gruyère cheese (about 1³/₄ cups)

1 cup milk

1 cup crème fraîche

2 eggs, lightly beaten

¹/₂ teaspoon salt

¹/₄ teaspoon freshly ground black pepper

MAKES ONE 11-INCH TART

QUICHE AU FROMAGE BLEU, POIRE, ET NOIX

Blue Cheese, Pear, and Walnut Quiche

Blue cheese, pears, and walnuts often show up together in salads, but it's an unusual combination for quiche. Still, it's one I'm very fond of. As with all the quiches we make at Boulangerie Bay Bread, it's in the French style: fairly thin, with not much custard relative to the other ingredients. Use well-ripened, flavorful pears, even if they don't look good, and feel free to adjust the amount of cheese to suit your taste. Pine nuts can also be used in place of the walnuts. Serve this with a simple salad of frisée *tossed with a shallot vinaigrette.*

1 chilled, unbaked, 11-inch Pâte Brisée tart shell (page 59)

2 ripe pears, preferably Bartlett (peeling is optional), halved, cored, stemmed, and sliced lengthwise 1/4 inch thick

4 ounces blue cheese, crumbled (about 1 cup)

1/2 cup walnut halves, toasted and coarsely chopped

1/2 cup milk

1/2 cup crème fraîche

1 egg, lightly beaten

1/2 teaspoon salt

1/4 teaspoon freshly ground black pepper

MAKES ONE 11-INCH TART

1. Preheat oven to 425°. Place the chilled tart shell on a parchment paper–lined baking sheet. Arrange the pear slices, cheese, and 1/4 cup of the walnuts in the bottom of the tart shell. In a small bowl, whisk together the milk, crème fraîche, egg, salt, and pepper. Pour milk mixture over the filling and sprinkle the remaining 1/4 cup walnuts on top. Bake immediately until just set, 30 to 40 minutes. Let cool in the pan, on a wire rack, for 30 minutes before serving.

TARTELETTE AU SAUMON FUMÉ, POIREAUX, ET CITRON

Smoked Salmon, Leek, and Lemon Tartlets

This is a lighter tasting and more delicate alternative to quiche, because it's made without eggs. It would be a good choice for a summertime brunch, accompanied by a glass of sparkling wine and a simple ripe tomato salad.

1. Preheat oven to 425°. Place the chilled tartlet shells on a parchment paper–lined baking sheet.

2. In a large sauté pan, melt butter over medium-low heat. Add leeks and cook, stirring often, until tender, about 10 minutes; do not allow the leeks to brown. Transfer to a medium bowl and let cool.

3. Add the crème fraîche and lemon juice to the cooled leeks and mix well. Season to taste with black pepper. Divide the leek mixture evenly among the tartlet shells. Bake until the filling is just set, about 15 minutes. Remove the tartlets from the oven, top each with slices of smoked salmon, dividing evenly, and 1 or 2 slices of lemon. Drizzle with olive oil and return to oven. Bake until the salmon is pale pink and firm, about 5 minutes. Serve hot or at room temperature.

6 chilled, unbaked, 4-inch Pâte Brisée tartlet shells (page 59)

1 ounce (2 tablespoons) unsalted butter

2 large leeks, white parts only, trimmed, washed, and coarsely chopped

6 tablespoons crème fraîche

2 tablespoons fresh lemon juice

Freshly ground black pepper

4 ounces thinly sliced smoked salmon

$^1/_2$ lemon, thinly sliced crosswise and seeded

$1^1/_2$ teaspoons olive oil

MAKES SIX TARTLETS

TARTE aux CHAMPIGNONS et FROMAGE de CHÈVRE

Wild Mushroom and Goat Cheese Tart

This is a nice fall recipe that makes a substantial first course or a light main dish. It's really as simple as mushrooms, crème fraîche, and goat cheese baked on a flaky pastry shell. You can use any kind of fresh mushroom that holds its shape when cooked. The recipe works equally well with inexpensive button or cremini mushrooms as well as the fancier varieties, like oyster mushrooms or chanterelles.

1 pound fresh mushrooms, such as cremini and/or chanterelles

1 tablespoon unsalted butter

2 tablespoons olive oil

Salt and freshly ground black pepper

1 chilled, unbaked, 11-inch Pâte Brisée tart shell (page 59)

³/₄ cup crème fraîche

8-ounce goat cheese log, cut crosswise into ¹/₄-inch rounds

¹/₄ cup chopped fresh chives, plus extra for garnish

MAKES ONE 11-INCH TART

1. Slice the mushrooms, setting aside the 12 most attractive slices to garnish the top of the tart. In a large sauté pan, melt the butter and olive oil over medium-high heat. Add the mushrooms and cook, stirring often, until almost all of the liquid the mushrooms have given off has evaporated, about 10 minutes. Season with salt and pepper. Let cool.

2. Preheat oven to 425°. Place the chilled tart shell on a parchment paper–lined baking sheet. Spread ¹/₂ cup of the crème fraîche evenly in the bottom of the tart shell. Top the crème fraîche with the sautéed mushrooms and cover with the slices of goat cheese. Arrange the 12 reserved mushroom slices on the top of the goat cheese, season with salt and pepper, and sprinkle with ¹/₄ cup chives. Dollop the remaining ¹/₄ cup crème fraîche evenly on top of the tart. Bake immediately until the crust is golden and the filling is bubbling, 25 to 30 minutes. Let cool in the pan, on a wire rack. Serve warm with extra chopped chives sprinkled on top.

CROQUE MONSIEUR

Ham and Cheese Melt

Croque Monsieur *is the grilled cheese sandwich of France. At home, it's usually made in a pan on the stove-top, just as people do in the States. But in restaurants in France, they pile more cheese on top and melt it under the broiler. Sometimes they will add a fried egg on top of that and call it* Croque Madame. *When we started making* Croque Monsieur *at Boulangerie Bay Bread, we found that it dried out too quickly and didn't hold up well in the display case. Then we remembered how my wife Virginie's mother, who runs a bar in Dijon, makes her version with a little crème fraîche inside. We decided to go one step further and do ours with a rich béchamel.* Voilà! *Problem solved: a moist, gooey, super-satisfying* Croque Monsieur. *People always ask what our secret is. Now you know.*

1. To prepare the béchamel: In a medium saucepan combine the milk and cream and cook over medium heat until hot. Meanwhile, in a separate medium saucepan, melt the butter over medium heat. Whisk the flour into the butter and cook, whisking constantly, until the roux bubbles, but doesn't brown, about 2 minutes. Add the hot milk mixture, salt, and pepper to the roux, whisking constantly, and bring to a boil. Continue to boil, whisking constantly, until the roux thickens, about 2 minutes. Remove from the heat and whisk 1 cup of the hot sauce into the egg yolks, and then whisk this tempered egg mixture into the remaining sauce in the saucepan. Press a piece of plastic wrap directly on the surface of the sauce. Allow sauce to cool and thicken slightly. (The cooled béchamel can be kept, covered and refrigerated, up to 5 days. Bring to room temperature before proceeding.)

2. Preheat the oven to 400°. Place the *pain de mie* on a work surface. Using a small spatula, spread a thin layer (about 1 tablespoon) of the béchamel sauce on each slice of *pain de mie*. Top each of 4 bread slices with one-quarter of the ham and ¼ cup of the shredded Gruyère. Turn the remaining bread slices, sauce side down, over cheese-topped slices. Spread the top surface of the sandwich with another thin layer of béchamel sauce. Pile ¾ cup of the remaining Gruyère on top of each sandwich. Transfer the sandwiches to a parchment paper–lined baking sheet, and bake until the cheese is nicely melted, about 10 minutes. If desired, place under the broiler to brown a bit, about 1 minute. Serve, hot, with a little green salad or coleslaw on the side.

BÉCHAMEL

1 cup milk

¹/₂ cup heavy cream or crème fraîche

2 ounces (4 tablespoons) unsalted butter

¹/₄ cup all-purpose flour

¹/₂ teaspoon salt

¹/₄ teaspoon freshly ground black pepper

2 extra-large egg yolks, set aside in a large bowl

8 slices Pain de Mie (page 30) or other firm white bread

8 ounces thinly sliced, good-quality ham (about 8 slices)

12 ounces shredded Gruyère cheese (about 4 cups, lightly packed)

MAKES FOUR MELTS

TARTINE DE JAMBON SEC AUX FIGUES

Ham and Fig Open-Faced Sandwich

This tartine *was inspired by the much-loved combination of prosciutto and fruit. In the United States, people are becoming more familiar with Serrano ham, Spain's version of prosciutto that is salt-cured in the same way. I love how it tastes with the organic fresh figs we get from Rick Knoll's farm in Brentwood. If fresh figs are out of season, you may garnish with more of the sliced dried figs used to make the fig purée. The purée in this recipe is fantastic on its own as a jam for toast or as an accompaniment to grilled or roasted pork. You also can whisk it with a little oil and balsamic vinegar to make a simple, sweet vinaigrette for salad greens.*

FIG PURÉE

4 ounces dried Turkish figs or Knoll Farms semi-dried figs, chopped

$1/2$ cup water

1 tablespoon fresh lemon

6 slices, each $1/2$-inch-thick, Pan au Levain (page 23), grilled or lightly toasted

12 ounces Fourme d'Ambert, Bleu d'Auvergne, or Roquefort cheese, crumbled

$1/4$ pound thinly sliced Serrano ham (12 to 18 slices)

9 to 12 fresh Black Mission figs, thinly sliced

2 tablespoons very thinly sliced fresh basil leaves

2 tablespoons extra virgin olive oil

MAKES SIX SANDWICHES

1. To prepare the fig purée: In a small saucepan, combine the dried figs and water. Bring to a boil over medium heat. Remove from the heat and let stand 30 minutes, until softened. In a blender or food processor, combine the figs, with their liquid, and lemon juice; purée until smooth, adding a little more warm water if necessary to form a smooth purée. (The fig purée can be kept in an airtight container in the refrigerator, up to 1 week.)

2. Spread the toasted bread slices with the fig purée, dividing evenly; top each with an equal amount of the cheese. Place the *tartines* on a baking sheet and bake in the oven until hot, 5 to 10 minutes. Transfer the *tartines* to a serving platter, or individual serving plates, and garnish each with 2 to 3 slices Serrano ham, some of the fresh fig slices, a sprinkle of basil, and a drizzle of olive oil. Serve immediately.

TARTINE NIÇOISE
Niçoise Open-Faced Sandwich

This popular sandwich from Boulangerie Bay Bread makes a great light meal all by itself. Think of it as Salade Niçoise *on toast—the salad is piled on an extra-large crouton, so you can just pick the whole thing up and eat it. Tiny niçoise olives are traditional, but warn your guests to watch out for the pits! We also like the flavor of kalamata olives for this.*

1. To prepare the tuna salad: In a medium bowl, combine the tuna, potato, onion, roasted pepper, olive oil, and vinegar; mix well. Season to taste with salt and pepper. The salad can be kept, covered and refrigerated, up to 24 hours. Bring to room temperature before proceeding.

2. To assemble the *tartines*, spread each piece of bread with 1 tablespoon of the mayonnaise and top with one-quarter of the tuna salad. Arrange some of the olives and radish slices nicely on top of each *tartine*, dividing equally. Place a tiny dollop of mayonnaise on each of the egg halves. Transfer the *tartines* to a serving platter, or individual serving plates, with the egg halves alongside.

ROASTED PEPPERS

Many of our recipes call for "roasted red bell peppers." This ingredient is a staple of any Mediterranean menu. We remove the skin of bell peppers, as it is tough and chewy when cooked. This is an easy process, but there are more ways than one to skin a pepper!

Method 1: Using a gas stove, place the bell pepper on a mesh tray over high heat, and cook, turning frequently, until all sides are evenly blistered.

Method 2: Place the bell peppers on a lightly oiled baking sheet and broil directly under the flame of a preheated broiler, turning several times until all sides are evenly blistered.

Method 3: Roast peppers in the oven on a baking sheet at 400° for about 30 minutes, until evenly blistered. Turn several times while roasting; the sides touching the pan will brown and blister more quickly.

Whichever method you use, immediately place the bell peppers in a covered bowl or in a plastic bag. Let steam for 15 minutes. When cool, gently peel or rub the skins off with your fingers. Resist the impulse to rinse, as rinsing removes some of the great roasted flavor. After removing the skin, core and seed the bell peppers, saving their very flavorful juices, and reserve for use in the recipes.

TUNA SALAD

2 cans (6 ounces each) best quality, water- or oil-packed tuna, depending on your preference

5 small (or 3 medium) new red creamer potatoes, boiled and cut into small cubes

1/2 cup diced red onion

1 roasted red bell pepper, diced (about 1 1/2 cup)

1/2 cup olive oil

3 tablespoons red wine vinegar

Salt and freshly ground black pepper

5 tablespoons mayonnaise plus 1 tablespoon for garnish

4 slices, each 1/2-inch-thick, Pain au Levain (page 23), lightly toasted

24 small niçoise olives

16 small red radishes, thinly sliced

4 hard-boiled eggs, peeled and cut in half

MAKES FOUR SANDWICHES

TARTINE DE POIVRONS ROUGES ET FROMAGE DE CHÈVRE

Sweet Pepper and Goat Cheese Open-Faced Sandwich

The heart and soul of this sandwich is the pipérade, *the famous Basque dish of peppers and onions braised in olive oil. In this dish, the skins are left on the peppers. Our version goes perfectly with the tangy richness of goat cheese. It also makes a great side dish with grilled tuna or roast chicken, and at one of our restaurants, Le Petit Robert, we also like to use it as an omelet filling.*

BRAISED PEPPERS

2 tablespoons olive oil

1 yellow onion, thinly sliced

1 pasilla chile, seeded and julienned

2 red bell peppers, seeded and julienned

2 yellow bell peppers, seeded and julienned

2 garlic cloves, minced

1 teaspoon salt

1/4 teaspoon freshly cracked black pepper

1 teaspoon minced fresh thyme

1/4 cup dry white wine

6 slices, each 1/2-inch-thick, Pain au Levain (page 23), lightly toasted

10 ounces crottin or another semi-soft goat cheese, cut into 12 slices, each 1/4-inch thick

3 tablespoons extra virgin olive oil

2 tablespoons chopped fresh parsley

MAKES SIX SANDWICHES

1. To prepare the braised peppers: In a large sauté pan, heat the oil over medium heat. Add the onions and cook until translucent, about 5 minutes. Add the pasilla chile, red and yellow bell peppers, and garlic. Cook, stirring occasionally, until the peppers begin to soften and release some of their juices, about 3 minutes. Add 1/2 teaspoon salt, pepper, and thyme and continue cooking until the juices have evaporated. Add the wine and cook, stirring to dissolve the sticky pepper juices on the bottom of the pan, until the wine has evaporated, about 2 minutes. Remove from the heat, season to taste with salt and pepper, and let cool to room temperature. The peppers taste best the day they are made, but they can be kept, covered and refrigerated, up to 2 days. If the peppers have been refrigerated, return to room temperature before proceeding.

2. Preheat the oven to 400°. Place the toasted bread on a parchment paper–lined baking sheet. Divide the braised peppers evenly among the toasts and top each with 2 slices of the cheese. Bake until the cheese is melted, 6 to 8 minutes. If desired, place under the broiler to brown a bit, about 1 minute. To serve, cut each *tartine* in half diagonally, and place on a plate. Drizzle with olive oil and garnish with a sprinkle of parsley.

TARTINE DE LA FORÊT

Open-Faced Mushroom Sandwich

We came up with this mushroom sandwich for our customers looking for a hearty vegetarian lunch or snack. I recommend making plenty of extra roasted peppers and keeping them in the refrigerator. Once you have a supply on hand, you can dig in and use them as a condiment with just about anything—especially sandwiches, omelets, and salads.

4 red bell peppers, roasted and peeled (see sidebar, page 71)

4 cloves garlic, sliced as thinly as possible

Salt and freshly ground black pepper

1/2 cup olive oil

4 large portobello mushrooms, cut into 3/4-inch slices

4 slices, each 1/2-inch-thick, Pain au Levain (page 23), lightly toasted

8 ounces goat cheese

8 ounces sliced Emmenthaler cheese (12 slices)

MAKES FOUR SANDWICHES

1. Preheat oven to 400°. Cut the roasted peppers into 1/2-inch-thick strips. Place in a shallow roasting pan and sprinkle with the garlic slices. Roast until the garlic is lightly toasted and golden brown, about 5 minutes. Transfer the garlic and pepper strips to a small bowl and season to taste with salt and pepper. Cover the peppers with 6 tablespoons of the olive oil. Let marinate, covered and refrigerated, for at least 6 hours and up to 1 week. Bring to room temperature before proceeding.

2. To prepare the mushrooms: In a large sauté pan, heat the remaining 2 tablespoons olive oil over medium-high heat. Add the mushroom slices and cook until golden brown and their liquid has evaporated, 6 to 8 minutes. Season to taste with salt and pepper. The mushrooms can be kept, covered and refrigerated, up to 2 days. Bring to room temperature before proceeding.

3. To assemble the *tartines:* Preheat the broiler. Place the toast slices on a nonstick or parchment paper–lined baking sheet. Spread a thick layer of goat cheese on each of the 4 slices. Divide the mushrooms and peppers evenly among the 4 slices, and then top each with 2 slices of Emmenthaler. Broil the *tartines* 6 to 8 inches from the heat, until the cheese starts to melt and the sandwich is warmed through, 3 to 4 minutes. Slice the *tartine* in half, diagonally, and serve immediately with a little salad on the side.

TARTINE "ROSTIE" AU FROMAGE BLANC, ANCHOIS MARINÉS, ET ONION ROUGE

Rye "Rostie" with Fromage Blanc, Salt-Cured Anchovies, and Slivers of Red Onion

For this tartine, *you make an herbed* fromage blanc, *spread it on slices of rye bread grilled in butter, and top it with anchovies and onions. If you're afraid of anchovies, this would be a good way to get over that, especially if you buy really nice ones from a specialty food store. The* fromage blanc *spread is great on its own with slices of baguette or crackers.*

1. To prepare the herbed *fromage blanc:* In the bowl of an electric mixer fitted with the paddle attachment, combine the *fromage blanc,* cream, shallots, garlic, herbs, olive oil, vinegars, *piment d'Espelette,* and ginger on low speed until well mixed. Set aside. (The *fromage blanc* mixture can be kept, covered and refrigerated, up to 3 days.)

2. Spread both sides of the bread with butter. Heat a large sauté pan over medium heat. When the pan is hot, add the bread and cook, turning as needed, until golden brown on both sides. Transfer toasts to serving plates. Spread each toast with some of the *fromage blanc* mixture, dividing equally. Divide the onion slices and anchovy fillets evenly among the 6 sandwiches. Drizzle each with a little of the olive oil and garnish with a sprinkling of chervil. Serve immediately.

HERBED FROMAGE BLANC

1 pound fromage blanc
  (40 percent fat)

$1/4$ cup heavy cream

2 teaspoons minced shallots

$1/2$ teaspoon minced garlic

$1/2$ cup chopped fresh herbs, such as
  a combination of tarragon, parsley,
  chervil, chives, basil

1 tablespoon extra virgin olive oil

1 teaspoon red wine vinegar

1 teaspoon balsamic vinegar

$1/2$ teaspoon piment d'Espelette
  (see page 78)

1 pinch ground ginger

6 slices, each $1/2$-inch-thick, rye
  bread

1 ounce (2 tablespoons) of the
  tastiest European-style butter you
  can find

1 red onion, sliced very thin

36 canned, salt-cured anchovies,
  filleted and rinsed

Extra virgin olive oil, for drizzling

Chervil sprigs, for garnish

MAKES SIX SANDWICHES

TARTINE DE SAUMON FUMÉ

Smoked Salmon Open-Faced Sandwich

We like combinations that are simple, but still offer many layers of taste and texture, so you stay interested and want to keep eating. This tartine is a good example of that idea. It has the intense, smoky quality of the fish, the wet crunch of cucumbers, the bright tartness of lemon, and the richness of crème fraîche to hold it all together. It's a good choice for a light summer lunch or a picnic.

1 cup crème fraîche

2 tablespoons fresh lemon juice

Salt and freshly ground black pepper

4 slices, each ¹/₂-inch-thick, Pain au Levain (page 23), lightly toasted

1 small English cucumber, peeled and very thinly sliced crosswise

12 ounces (12 slices) smoked salmon, gravlax, or smoked trout

Chopped fresh dill or parsley, for garnish

1 chopped shallot, for serving

MAKES FOUR SANDWICHES

1. In a small bowl, combine the crème fraîche and lemon juice, and mix well. Season with salt and pepper to taste. Top each of the 4 toasted bread slices with ¹/₄ cup of the crème fraîche mixture. Top each with the cucumber and smoked salmon slices, evenly dividing among the sandwiches. Garnish with a sprinkling of the dill or parsley. Transfer to a serving plate and serve with the chopped shallots, on the side, and a little salad, if desired.

TARTINE DE FOIE GRAS POÊLÉ AUX COINGS CONFITS

Seared Duck Foie Gras with Quince Gelée Open-Faced Sandwich

This is definitely a top-shelf tartine. Foie gras—a fantastic extravagance—is best when presented in simple ways, and the sweetness and acidity of the apple-quince gelée in this recipe is all you need to bring out its rich flavor. You don't need much foie gras for this—just a few thin slices on each tartine. The gelée is wonderful as a breakfast jam or served at the end of a meal with a salty, semi-firm cheese, such as manchego. If quinces are not available, you can substitute apples, such as Granny Smiths.

1. To prepare the quince *gelée:* In a medium saucepan, combine the quinces, liqueur, sugar, water, pectin, and lemon juice. Cook over medium-low heat, stirring occasionally, until the quinces become translucent, about 20 to 30 minutes. Let cool briefly, then transfer the mixture to a blender and purée until smooth. Let cool completely. (Placed in an airtight glass jar or food container, the quince *gelée* can be kept, covered and refrigerated, up to 5 days.)

2. Melt the duck fat in a large, nonstick sauté pan over medium heat. When the pan is hot, add the bread and cook, turning as needed, until golden brown on both sides. Set aside.

3. Season the slices of foie gras with salt and pepper and dredge lightly in flour. Heat a large sauté pan over medium-high heat. Add the foie gras and quickly sear the first side until nicely browned, 1 to 1½ minutes. (This is the side that will be facing up on the finished *tartine* and should have the most color.) Turn the foie gras and finish cooking until just medium rare, ½ to 1 minute longer. The cooking time will depend on the thickness of your slice and the temperature of your burner, so watch closely. Do not overcook the foie gras.

4. Spread each piece of toast with about ½ tablespoon of the quince *gelée* and place on a serving plate. Lay 2 pieces of the seared foie gras on each toast, and sprinkle with some *Sel de Guerande*, cracked pepper, and chopped chives. Serve immediately.

QUINCE GELÉE

2 to 3 quinces, peeled, cored, and sliced ¼-inch thick

1 cup quince liqueur or apple brandy

½ cup sugar

¼ cup water

½ teaspoon dry pectin

Juice of 1 lemon

1 ounce (2 tablespoons) duck fat or the tastiest European-style butter you can find

6 slices, each ½-inch-thick, Pain au Levain (page 23)

6 ounces fresh foie gras, cut into 12 slices, each ½-inch-thick

Salt and freshly ground black pepper

Flour, for dredging

Sel de Guerande or other sea salt, for sprinkling

Cracked black pepper

1 bunch chives, finely chopped

MAKES SIX SANDWICHES

LE SANDWICH AU FROMAGE DE CHÈVRE, POIVRON, ET PIMENT D'ESPELETTE

Goat Cheese, Red Pepper, and Piment d'Espelette Sandwich

The most exciting ingredient in this sandwich is the one that's proportionately the smallest: piment d'Espelette. *It's an essential seasoning in Basque cooking, a powder ground from a prized type of chile pepper grown and sun-dried in southwestern France. Compared to most chiles,* piment d'Espelette *is fairly mild and a bit sweet— just the thing to bring out the sweetness of the roasted peppers and cut through the creaminess of the goat cheese. If you can't find the little containers labeled IGO, our favorite brand,* piment d'Espelette, *you may substitute a mixture of 1 tablespoon paprika and ¼ teaspoon cayenne pepper.*

---

6 ounces fresh goat cheese, at room temperature

2 tablespoons heavy cream

1 very fresh baguette (about 32 inches long)

2 roasted red bell peppers, julienned (see sidebar, page 71)

Piment d'Espelette, for garnish

MAKES FOUR SANDWICHES

1. In a small bowl, combine the goat cheese and heavy cream. Mix until it forms a spreadable consistency. Slice the baguettes crosswise into 4 equal portions, about 8 inches each, and then slice each portion in half, horizontally. Spread each of the bottom pieces with one-quarter of the cheese mixture. Divide the roasted red peppers evenly among the 4 sandwiches and then sprinkle each with some of the fantastic, slightly sweet *piment d'Espelette.* Cover with the baguette tops and serve.

SANDWICH JAMBON, BEURRE, ET FROMAGE

Ham, Butter, and Cheese Sandwich

You can find a simple ham and cheese sandwich all over the world. If you're in France, chances are this is the type you will find. A mere three ingredients, but just right in every way. These are great with a little glass of simple red wine.

1. Slice the baguettes crosswise into four equal portions, about 8 inches each, and then slice each portion in half, horizontally. Spread the cut surfaces with a thin layer of butter. Arrange 1 slice of the ham and one slice of cheese on each of the bottom pieces of the baguette, folding as necessary so the ham and cheese won't stick out of the sandwiches too much. Cover with the baguette tops and serve.

1 very fresh baguette (about 32-inches long)

The tastiest European-style butter you can find, for spreading

4 ounces (4 very thin slices) of the very best ham available

4 ounces (4 very thin slices) of the very best Gruyère available

MAKES FOUR SANDWICHES

LE SANDWICH AU SAUCISSON ET BEURRE

Salami and Butter Sandwich

Just like the Sandwich Jambon, Beurre, et Fromage, *this is the real thing. Use a dry, hard salami, sliced paper thin, and don't skip the* cornichons—sacre bleu! *I like a little glass of very sharp sauvignon blanc with these.*

1. Slice the baguettes crosswise into 4 equal portions, about 8 inches each, and then slice each portion in half, horizontally. Spread the cut surfaces with a thin layer of butter. Arrange about 10 slices of the saucisson on each of the bottom pieces of baguette, and then top with 6 *cornichon* halves, placed down the length of each sandwich. Cover with the baguette tops and serve.

1 very fresh baguette (about 32 inches long)

The tastiest European-style butter you can find, for spreading

8 ounces thinly sliced, very dry saucisson or salami (about 40 slices)

12 cornichons, sliced in half lengthwise

MAKES FOUR SANDWICHES

LES SPECIALITÉS DE LA MAISON
House Specialties

The "specialties" you will find in this chapter are very special indeed, and very close to my heart. Though you might find them in a *pâtisserie* in Paris, they are more the kind of thing you'd see in a small-town boulangerie like the one I apprenticed in—pastries of the baker more than the pastry chef. For the most part, they are unadorned, honest, and simple. Many are also the stuff of home bakers. When I was growing up, every mom seemed to know instinctively how to make madeleines, meringues, and a simple pound cake. Many are centuries-old regional or holiday specialties as well. If you want to experience the flavors and joys of true traditional French baking, this is a great place to start. In fact, when we opened our Boulangerie Bay Bread in San Francisco, that's just what we did. The following specialties were the first pastries we sold because they felt the closest to my roots. And to this day, they remain among the most popular.

CANNELÉS DE BORDEAUX

Cannelés from Bordeaux

These extraordinary little confections are a specialty of Bordeaux, where nuns were said to have created them more than 200 years ago using the flour they salvaged from the holds of sailing ships anchored in the Port de la Lune. I like to call them "portable crème brûlée" because they contrast a crunchy caramelized exterior with a moist, custardy center. This recipe is a bit particular. You really need authentic copper cannelé molds and you really do need to coat them with beeswax (which you can find at some health-food stores and farmers' markets). The wax makes the unmolding easier, and—most important—gives the cannelés their distinctive, crunchy crust. Make sure you let the batter rest for the full twelve hours. The best way to eat these is with a cup of strong coffee. You could also serve them as a dessert, cut in half and drizzled with caramel sauce.

3 cups milk

¹/₂ vanilla bean, split lengthwise and scraped

7¹/₂ ounces (3 tablespoons plus ³/₄ cup) unsalted butter

1 cup sugar

²/₃ cup pastry flour

1 extra-large egg yolk

2 extra-large eggs

3 tablespoons dark rum

3 ounces beeswax, finely chopped (about ¹/₃ cup)

MAKES EIGHTEEN CANNELÉS

1. In a small saucepan, combine the milk, vanilla bean, and its scrapings. Bring the milk to the scalding point over medium-high heat, then remove the pan from the heat and add the 3 tablespoons of butter. Set aside to cool to lukewarm.

2. In a large bowl, whisk together the sugar and flour. In a separate small bowl, whisk together the egg yolk, eggs, and rum. Whisk the egg mixture into the sugar and flour mixture, then whisk in the lukewarm milk mixture. Strain into a container; cover and refrigerate for at least 12 hours.

3. To prepare molds for baking, melt the beeswax in a saucepan over low heat. Add the remaining ³/₄ cup butter to the melted wax and stir until the butter is melted. Remove the mixture from the heat and, using a narrow pastry brush, carefully coat the inside of 18, 2 x 1-inch *cannelés* molds. (Dedicate this brush to *cannelés*-making because the wax will get into the brush.) If the wax mixture starts to set up or thicken, return it to the heat for a moment until it thins.

4. Remove the batter from the refrigerator at least 1 hour before baking it. Preheat the oven to 425°. Place the waxed *cannelés* molds on a heavy baking sheet with a rim to prevent any wax and butter that melts from the molds from dripping onto the bottom of your oven and creating a fire hazard. Fill the molds three-quarters full with the batter, whisking the batter frequently and well to ensure that the sugar and flour remain evenly distributed.

5. Bake for about 50 minutes, or until the surface of the *cannelés* is dark brown. Remove from the oven, being very careful not to spill any of the hot wax on yourself. (It is wise to keep children and pets out of the kitchen during this part of the process.) Using tongs or an old towel, pick up each mold and tap it upside down to remove the *cannelés*. If it doesn't come out after a few taps, use a paring knife to loosen it from the sides. And . . . *voila!* Serve warm from the oven.

MADELEINES

Madeleines

Proust may have been the one to give these little cakes literary immortality, but if you ask anyone who grew up in France, they will have plenty of childhood madeleine memories of their own. I think right away of drinking hot chocolate with a madeleine—usually the supermarket kind, which in France are actually great—floating on the surface like a little boat. And that's still my standard: If it doesn't float, if it doesn't bob back up to the surface when you sink it with your spoon, and if it doesn't have a lump on top, it's not a true madeleine. In fact, I believe the right way to serve madeleines is scallop-side down, so you can see the lump. My trick for ensuring a proper lump: Pop the filled molds in the freezer for ten minutes just before you bake your madeleines. I still think they're best with hot chocolate, but I also like them with coffee or tea or warm, with ice cream.

3 cups plus 2 tablespoons all-purpose flour

2^1/$_2$ teaspoons baking powder

8 extra-large eggs

2 teaspoons vanilla extract

14^1/$_2$ ounces (1^1/$_2$ cups plus 5 tablespoons) unsalted butter, melted and kept warm

2^3/$_4$ cups powdered sugar

^{1}/$_4$ cup firmly packed light brown sugar

3 tablespoons honey

MAKES THIRTY-FIVE PLAIN MADELEINES

1. Preheat the oven to 375°. If you're using nonstick madeleine pans, spray them with vegetable oil spray. If your pans are not nonstick, simply brush each well with melted butter, allow to set (this keeps it from absorbing too much flour; place the pans in the refrigerator if the room is warm), then dust with all-purpose flour, tapping out the excess.

2. In a medium bowl, whisk together the flour and baking powder. In another medium bowl, whisk together the eggs and vanilla extract. In the bowl of an electric mixer fitted with the whisk attachment, beat all the warm butter with the powdered sugar on low speed until smooth and free of lumps. Add the brown sugar and honey and mix until smooth, scraping down the sides and bottom of the bowl as needed. Add half of the flour mixture to the butter-sugar mixture. Mix on low speed until smooth. With the mixer still on low speed, gradually add all of the egg mixture, scraping down the sides and bottom of the bowl as needed. Once the mixture is well combined, stop the mixer and add the remaining flour mixture. Mix on low speed just until all the flour is incorporated. At this point, the batter may be used immediately, but it is best if refrigerated for at least 4 hours (and up to 2 days) in an airtight container before baking.

3. If there is time, bring the batter to room temperature before using (it will be easier to work with). Fill each well three-quarters full using either a pastry bag or a small scoop.

4. Bake in the center of the oven for 22 to 26 minutes, or until golden brown. Immediately unmold by inverting the pans, tapping them if needed against a work surface. Transfer the madeleines to a wire rack to cool completely (don't let them cool in the pan or they may stick.)

For chocolate madeleines: Set aside 2 cups of your finished batter. In a small bowl, whisk together ¼ cup sifted, unsweetened cocoa powder and ¼ cup warm, melted butter. Add the reserved batter and whisk until combined. Fill one side of the prepared molds with the chocolate batter and the other side with the plain batter. Garnish with as many chocolate chips as you desire.

MAKES TWENTY-EIGHT CHOCOLATE MADELEINES PLUS
TWENTY-ONE PLAIN MADELEINES

For hazelnut madeleines: Toast, skin, and finely chop ¼ cup hazelnuts. Sprinkle each madeleine with some of the hazelnuts before baking.

MAKES THIRTY-FIVE HAZELNUT MADELEINES

QUATRE-QUARTS au CITRON
Lemon Pound Cake

Quatre-quarts *means "four quarters," so named because, like any traditional pound cake, it was originally made with equal parts butter, sugar, egg, and flour. This is a buttery version in the style of Normandy, Brittany, and the Charentes near La Rochelle, the great butter-producing regions of France. I sometimes call it a "five-quarters" cake, because the addition of lemon is really not traditional. We like how the lemon syrup makes it extra moist and balances the flavor. But you can also omit the syrup and you'll have an excellent everyday pound cake that is a little more dense and sturdy—what I think of as a gâteau de voyage—a cake that travels well. I like it for breakfast, perhaps with a little "milk jam" (the French version of dulce de leche caramel sauce), or with coffee or tea in the afternoon. If you're serving a fruit salad, it's perfect on the side for soaking up the juice. It's helpful to line the pan completely with parchment, especially in the corners, to keep the cake from sticking.*

CAKE

2 cups all-purpose flour

1/4 teaspoon salt

2 1/4 teaspoons baking powder

5 extra-large eggs

2 tablespoons milk

10 ounces (1 1/4 cups) unsalted
   butter, at room temperature

1 cup plus 6 tablespoons sugar

4 teaspoons freshly grated lemon
   zest

1 teaspoon lemon extract

LEMON SYRUP

1/2 cup water

1/2 cup sugar

3 tablespoons fresh lemon juice

MAKES ONE LARGE LOAF

1. Preheat the oven to 350°. Spray a 9 x 5 x 3-inch loaf pan with vegetable oil spray and line the sides of the pan with parchment paper, leaving a 1-inch overhang on each side to make for easier removal of the finished cake.

2. To make the cake: In a medium bowl, combine the flour, salt, and baking powder. In a small bowl, mix together the eggs and milk. In the bowl of an electric mixer fitted with the paddle attachment, cream together the butter, sugar, lemon zest, and lemon extract on low speed. Scrape down the sides and bottom of the bowl as needed. Add the dry ingredients to the mixing bowl in three additions, alternating with the milk mixture, mixing thoroughly and scraping after each addition. Transfer the batter to the prepared loaf pan and smooth surface.

3. Bake for 1 hour or until golden brown and a toothpick inserted in the center comes out clean.

4. While the cake is baking, make the lemon syrup: In a small saucepan, combine the water and sugar. Bring to a boil over high heat. Remove from the heat, and add the lemon juice, stirring to combine. Set aside while the cake finishes baking.

5. When the cake comes out of the oven, pour the syrup slowly over the hot cake. Let the cake cool in the pan set on a wire rack for 15 to 30 minutes. Invert the cake from the pan and place right side up on a serving plate. Wrapped airtight, the cake will keep for 5 days at room temperature or for 1 month in the freezer.

QUATRE-QUARTS au CHOCOLAT et à L'ORANGE
Chocolate-Orange Pound Cake

This is essentially a moist orange pound cake in which some of the batter is flavored with chocolate and marbled in. The marbling is a fun activity, so this is a great choice to make with kids. You can also make this cake without the orange syrup. Just pour yourself some Grand Marnier for dunking and drinking on the side.

1. Preheat the oven to 350°. Spray 1, 9 x 5 x 3-inch loaf pan or 3, 5¾ x 3 x 2-inch loaf pans with vegetable oil spray.

2. To make the cake: In a small heatproof bowl, melt the chocolate over a pan of boiling water, stirring occasionally. As soon as the chocolate has melted, remove the bowl from the heat and set aside. In a medium bowl, sift together the flour, baking powder, and salt. In the bowl of an electric mixer fitted with the paddle attachment, cream together the butter and sugar on low speed just until smooth, about 1 minute. Scrape down the sides and bottom of the bowl as needed. Add the sour cream, Grand Marnier liqueur, corn syrup, and orange zest. Mix on low speed until thoroughly combined, about 1 minute. Again, scrape down the sides and bottom of the bowl as needed. Add the flour mixture to the butter mixture in three additions, alternating with the eggs, mixing thoroughly and scraping down the sides and bottom of the bowl after each addition.

3. Using a flexible spatula, gradually mix one-third of the finished batter into the melted chocolate. Place the loaf pan(s) on a baking sheet. Spread the batter without chocolate into the prepared loaf pan(s), and then spread the chocolate batter over the plain batter. Marble the chocolate batter into the plain batter dragging a butter knife vertically through the two mixtures.

4. Bake for 1 hour and 10 minutes for one large loaf, or 40 to 50 minutes for three small loaves, or until a toothpick inserted in the center comes out clean.

5. While the cake is baking, make the syrup: In a small saucepan, combine the sugar and water. Bring to a boil over high heat. Remove from the heat and add the orange and lemon juices. Set aside.

6. When the cake comes out of the oven, pour the syrup slowly over the hot cake. Cool in the pan on a rack for 15 to 30 minutes. Invert the cake from the pan and place right-side up on a serving plate. Wrapped airtight, the cake will keep for 5 days at room temperature or for 1 month in the freezer.

CAKE

3 ounces bittersweet chocolate, finely chopped (about ¹/₃ cup)

2 cups pastry flour

2 teaspoons baking powder

¹/₄ teaspoon salt

10 ounces (1¹/₄ cups) unsalted butter, at room temperature

1 cup plus 2 tablespoons sugar

3 tablespoons sour cream

2 tablespoons Grand Marnier liqueur or orange juice

1 tablespoon light corn syrup

1 tablespoon freshly grated orange zest

4 extra-large eggs

SYRUP

¹/₂ cup sugar

¹/₂ cup water

¹/₄ cup fresh orange juice

2 teaspoons fresh lemon juice

MAKES ONE LARGE LOAF OR THREE SMALL LOAVES

PAIN D'ÉPICES
Spice Cake

This spice cake, with its dense crumb and intense flavor, is a specialty of the Burgundy region, especially the city of Dijon. Although as a tradition it's centuries old, it has the very modern-day appeal of being both vegan (no eggs or dairy products) and completely fat free. The cake is best when prepared a day ahead and allowed to sit overnight wrapped in plastic wrap. Tightly wrapped, it will keep for five days at room temperature. The recipe calls for a simple caramel that should be prepared at least one hour before the cake is mixed, as it needs to cool before using.

¹/₄ cup firmly packed dark brown sugar

1 tablespoon ground cinnamon

¹/₂ teaspoon ground ginger

¹/₄ teaspoon ground anise seed

¹/₄ teaspoon ground nutmeg

¹/₄ teaspoon ground coriander

¹/₈ teaspoon ground cloves

¹/₈ teaspoon ground allspice

1¹/₂ teaspoons baking soda

1¹/₂ teaspoons baking powder

¹/₄ teaspoon salt

³/₄ cup caramel (recipe follows), at room temperature

¹/₂ cup honey

1¹/₂ teaspoons vanilla extract

1³/₄ cups boiling water

2²/₃ cups rye flour

1¹/₃ cups pastry flour

CARAMEL FOR PAIN D'ÉPICES

³/₄ cup sugar

²/₃ cup water

MAKES ONE LARGE LOAF OR THREE SMALL LOAVES

1. Preheat the oven to 375°. Spray one 9 x 5 x 3-inch or three 5³/₄ x 3 x 2-inch loaf pans with vegetable oil spray.

2. In a large bowl, whisk together the brown sugar, cinnamon, ginger, aniseed, nutmeg, coriander, clove, allspice, baking soda, baking powder, and salt. Use your fingers to break up any small lumps in the baking soda. Add the cooled caramel, honey, and vanilla extract to the spice mixture and whisk until combined. Whisk in the boiling water, and then let this mixture stand for 30 seconds to allow the baking soda and baking powder to activate; the mixture will become foamy. Whisk the rye and pastry flours into the mixture until a smooth batter is formed. Pour the batter into the prepared pan(s).

3. Bake for 55 minutes for one large loaf, or 40 minutes for three small loaves, or until dark brown and the air is fragrant with spices. Cool in the pan for 15 minutes, then unmold the cake and cool it completely on a wire rack. Wrap the cooled cake in plastic wrap and let rest overnight before serving. The tightly wrapped cake will keep, at room temperature, up to 5 days.

CARAMEL FOR PAIN D'ÉPICES

1. In a small saucepan, combine the sugar and ¹/₃ cup of the water. Stir until all of the sugar is moistened. Place the saucepan over medium-high heat and, to ensure even cooking, swirl the pan gently as the sugar begins to color. Caramelize the sugar to dark golden brown, taking care that it doesn't burn. (Don't touch the sugar while it's caramelizing—it will cause a severe burn!)

2. Stop the caramelization by stirring the remaining ¹/₃ cup water into the pan. Be careful—adding the water to the hot caramel will cause steam and spitting. If needed, put the pan back on the heat and stir until smooth. Cool the caramel to room temperature.

3. When the caramel has cooled, stir in enough water to make ³/₄ cup for the *Pain d'Épices* recipe.

FINANCIERS

Brown Butter Hazelnut Cakes

In France, these rich, buttery nut cakes run a close second to madeleines in terms of popularity. Traditionally, they're made with ground almonds, but we give ours a special twist and a deeper, toastier flavor by using ground hazelnuts instead. The whole key to Financiers *is getting the brown butter right. It should be a true* beurre noisette—*a deep brown butter that smells like toasted hazelnuts, and the trick is to remove it from the heat a split-second before it burns.* Friand *or* Financier *molds are small, rectangular molds with angled sides, available at specialty cookware shops. They measure 4-inches long by 2-inches wide. You may substitute mini-muffin pans or madeleine pans.*

8 ounces (1 cup) unsalted butter

2¼ cups powdered sugar

½ cup plus 3 tablespoons all-purpose flour

3½ ounces (1 cup) finely ground hazelnuts

⅛ teaspoon salt

8 extra-large egg whites

½ teaspoon vanilla extract

1 cup fresh blackberries or raspberries

MAKES EIGHTEEN CAKES

1. To make the browned butter: In a 2-quart saucepan, melt the butter over low heat. Once the butter is melted, turn the heat up to medium and continue cooking, swirling the pan occasionally. At first the butter will bubble wildly, and then the solids will start to sink to the bottom of the pan and turn brown. When the butter is deep brown and smells nutty and delicious, it's ready. Be careful not to let it burn; the difference is a matter of seconds. Remove the pan from the heat and set aside in a warm place.

2. In the bowl of an electric mixer fitted with the whisk attachment, combine the powdered sugar, flour, hazelnuts, and salt on low speed. With the mixer off, pour in the hot browned butter, making sure to scrape the tasty brown bits off the bottom of the saucepan. Mix on low speed until combined. Still on low speed, slowly add the egg whites and vanilla extract and mix thoroughly, scraping down the sides and bottom of the bowl as necessary. Transfer the batter to an airtight container and refrigerate for about 1 hour or until firm. The batter can be kept in the refrigerator for up to 3 days.

3. To bake, preheat the oven to 375°. Arrange the nonstick 4 x 2-inch *friand* or *financier* molds on a cookie sheet and fill three-quarters full with batter. If using muffin pans, spray them with vegetable oil spray and fill them one-third full with batter. Top each with 2 to 3 berries of your choice.

4. Bake for 25 minutes, or until golden brown and springy to the touch. Cool for 5 minutes in pans, then unmold (if needed, run a knife around the edges) onto a wire rack. Dust with powdered sugar and serve warm or at room temperature. They are best the day they are baked.

CROQUETS BORDELAIS
Bordeaux Almond Cookies

These crunchy cookies are a specialty of the Médoc, Bordeaux's most famous wine region. They're a little like a once-baked biscotti, though much more buttery and delicate than their Italian cousins. Like biscotti, they're made for dipping. In Bordeaux, what they get dipped in most is wine—red, white, or Champagne. They're also great with a cup of tea or coffee. The dough needs to be frozen overnight, so a bit of preplanning is needed. You can keep the dough in the freezer for up to a week.

1. In a medium bowl, stir together the finely ground almonds, flour, baking powder, and salt; set aside. In the bowl of an electric mixer fitted with the paddle attachment, cream the butter and sugar on low speed just until smooth. Add the lemon zest and then the eggs, one at a time, scraping down the sides and bottom of the bowl after each addition. With the mixer on low speed, add the ground almond mixture to the mixing bowl and mix thoroughly, scraping down the sides and bottom of the bowl as necessary. Fold in the chopped almonds with a flexible spatula until evenly distributed. Place the dough in a mound on a piece of plastic wrap about 18-inches long, and pat the dough into a 9 x 6½-inch rectangle. Enclose the dough in the plastic wrap, smoothing the surface as you go by rubbing your hands along the plastic wrap. Put the dough package on a cookie sheet and place in the freezer to firm up overnight.

2. Preheat the oven to 375°. Remove the dough from the freezer and place it on a cutting surface. Using a ruler, mark 3-inch lengths along the 9-inch side of the dough. With a chef's knife, cutting crosswise straight down through the dough, cut the dough into three 3 x 6½-inch bars. Return two of the bars to the freezer to keep the dough firm. Place one bar widthwise on the cutting surface (so the shorter sides are along the top and bottom), and cut each bar crosswise into 1/2-inch slices. (You should have thirteen 3-inch-long cookies.) Repeat process to cut remaining frozen dough bars into slices. Line baking sheets with parchment paper. Arrange the slices on the parchment-lined baking sheets in two rows, a maximum of ten cookies per pan. With a pastry brush, brush the top of each cookie lightly with the egg wash.

3. Bake for 18 to 19 minutes or until golden brown. Carefully slide the parchment paper, with the cookies on it, off the cookie sheet and onto a wire rack to cool. As they cool, they set into a hard and crunchy cookie. The cookies can be kept in an airtight container for up to 5 days.

11 ounces (3 cups) finely ground almonds

1½ cups all-purpose flour

2 teaspoons baking powder

1 teaspoon salt

4¼ ounces (½ cup plus 1½ teaspoons) unsalted butter, at room temperature

1⅔ cups sugar

1 tablespoon freshly grated lemon zest

2 extra-large eggs

4 ounces (1 cup) whole almonds, toasted and coarsely chopped

1 egg, beaten, for egg wash

MAKES THIRTY-NINE COOKIES

CONGOLAIS

Light Coconut Macaroons

We love the coconut taste of the classic Congolais, *but their texture can sometimes be quite heavy. Ours are lighter than the traditional ones—somewhere between a flan and a macaroon. Unlike macaroons, though, these* Congolais *must be baked in some kind of mold to hold them together, not "free-form" on a baking sheet. We bake them in pyramid-shaped molds but muffin tins also work well, and you can play around with all kinds of other mold shapes. These are wonderful eaten warm the same day they are baked, and even better drizzled with a little chocolate sauce.*

---

2 cups whole milk

2 tablespoons honey

$^1/_3$ cup pastry flour

3 cups unsweetened dried shredded coconut

$^1/_2$ cup sugar

2$^1/_4$ teaspoons baking powder

3 extra-large eggs

MAKES TEN TO TWELVE COCONUT MACAROONS

1. Preheat the oven to 375° and spray a 12-cup muffin tin with vegetable oil spray.

2. In a small saucepan, heat the milk and honey just to the scalding point. Meanwhile, in a large bowl, combine the flour, coconut, sugar, and baking powder. In a small bowl, gently whisk the eggs to break up the yolks. Whisk the scalding milk mixture quickly into the flour mixture and then gradually whisk in the eggs until combined. (At this point, the batter can be stored in an airtight container in the refrigerator for 3 to 4 days before baking.)

3. Fill the muffin cups to the top with batter. Bake for 20 to 25 minutes or until the tops are light golden brown. Cool the *Congolais* in the pan for 10 minutes, then run a thin-bladed knife around the edges of the cups and turn them out of the pan. Cool completely on a wire rack, right-side up. They can be stored at room temperature, well wrapped, for up to 3 days.

Pictured: Congolais, Biscuits Bretons, and Croquets Bordelais

BISCUITS BRETONS

Butter Cookies from Brittany

Over the years, I've worked to arrive at a version of this cookie with the greatest possible amount of butter incorporated into the dough, in the style of Brittany, where butter is a national treasure. These cookies should be meltingly delicate and tender; take care not to overwork the dough, or they will become tough when baked. For a more rustic type of cookie, you can also roll a piece of the dough out into a big circle, brush it with egg wash, and score it in wedges with a fork before baking.

12 ounces (1¹/₂ cups) unsalted butter, at room temperature

1¹/₄ cups sugar

³/₄ teaspoon salt

1 extra-large egg

1 teaspoon vanilla extract

3 cups pastry flour

1 egg, beaten, for egg wash

MAKES ABOUT EIGHTY TINY COOKIES

1. In the bowl of an electric mixer fitted with the paddle attachment, cream the butter, sugar, and salt on low speed just until smooth. Scrape down the sides and bottom of the bowl as needed. The mixture should not have too much air incorporated into it. Slowly add the egg and vanilla extract with the mixer on low speed. Add the flour all at once and mix, scraping down the sides and bottom of the bowl once, just until combined. Do not overmix. Turn dough out onto a piece of plastic wrap and pat the dough into a ¹/₂-inch-thick rectangle. Enclose the dough with the plastic wrap and refrigerate until firm, about 1 hour, or freeze for up to 2 months.

2. Preheat the oven to 375°. On a lightly floured surface, roll out the dough until ¹/₄-inch thick. Using a 2-inch-diameter cookie cutter (we use a fluted cutter), cut dough into rounds, flouring the cutter as needed to prevent the cookies from sticking. Refrigerate the scraps and re-roll when firm. Place the cookies 1 inch apart on parchment paper–lined baking sheets. Using a pastry brush, lightly brush the top of each cookie with egg wash.

3. Bake the cookies for about 18 minutes or until golden brown. Transfer to a wire rack to cool. The cookies can be kept in an airtight container for a few days, but they are best eaten the day they are made.

MERINGUES À L'EAU DE ROSE
Rosewater Meringues

These make a great summertime dessert or snack to serve with fresh seasonal fruit. They can be flavored with all kinds of ingredients, like pistachio, raspberry, or coffee, and they make a nice gift to bring along when you're visiting friends. In France, they are eaten just as a snack or cookie—not a dessert—but don't let that stop you. Try breaking them up and layering them in a big goblet with sliced strawberries and softened vanilla ice cream.

1. Preheat the oven to 200°. Line baking sheets with parchment paper.

2. In the bowl of an electric mixer fitted with the whisk attachment, whip the egg whites on medium speed until foamy. Increase the speed to high and gradually add the granulated sugar. Continue to whip to stiff peaks—the whites should be firm and shiny. As soon as the egg whites have reached the desired consistency, add the rosewater and turn off the mixer. Using a flexible spatula, gently fold the powdered sugar into the meringue.

3. Fit a piping bag with a ⅝-inch, number 7, stainless steel round tip and fill the bag with the meringue. Pipe half-dollar-size disks onto the parchment-lined baking sheets, ½ inch apart. (Alternatively, use a tablespoon to scoop the meringue onto parchment-lined baking sheets, leaving a ½-inch space between each meringue.) Use the back of a soup spoon to gently flatten the meringues to remove peaks.

4. Bake meringues for approximately 1 hour, or until they lift off cleanly from the parchment paper and are almost completely dry. Transfer to a wire rack to cool completely. When cooled, the meringues should break crisply with no softness. The meringues can be kept in an airtight container at room temperature for at least a week.

For cocoa nib meringues: Omit the rosewater and fold in 2 tablespoons cocoa nibs with the sifted powdered sugar. Continue with the recipe at step 3.

For hazelnut meringues: Omit the rosewater and sift the powdered sugar with ½ cup finely ground hazelnuts. Fold into beaten egg whites as directed in step 2, and then continue with the recipe at step 3.

2 extra-large egg whites
¼ cup granulated sugar
1 tablespoon rosewater
½ cup powdered sugar, sifted

MAKES FORTY-FIVE MERINGUES

MACARONS DE ST.-ÉMILION

Macaroons from St.-Émilion

The bakeries in the beautiful medieval village of St.-Émilion in Bordeaux have been selling these light, chewy almond cookies for more than a century, and always in the same way: in a box, still sticking to their baking paper. We had special boxes made up for Boulangerie Bay Bread, so we could sell them just like that. They're delicate and simple, a little like Italian amaretti, but with a softer texture. Be sure to make the plain macaroon mix the day before baking them. Enjoy them as they do in St.-Émilion, with Champagne or lightly sparkling crémant, *or try them with coffee, tea, or hot chocolate. As the caption on our package says, "We wish them a very short life in their box."*

---

8 ounces almond paste, broken into pieces

¹/₄ cup plus 2 teaspoons granulated sugar

³/₄ cup powdered sugar, sifted

2 large egg whites

2 to 3 teaspoons cold water

MAKES ABOUT FORTY TINY MACAROONS

1. In the bowl of an electric mixer fitted with the paddle attachment, combine the almond paste and granulated sugar on medium speed until the mixture obtains the consistency of a fine meal, about 10 minutes, scraping down the sides and bottom of the bowl as needed. Add the powdered sugar and mix on low speed until well combined, about 5 minutes.

2. With the mixer still on low speed, add the egg whites very, very slowly—about a teaspoon at a time—making sure each addition of egg whites is incorporated before adding any more. Stop and scrape down the sides and bottom of the bowl midway through mixing. If there are any lumps, stop adding the egg whites and continue mixing until mixture is smooth. Resume adding the egg whites very, very slowly, until they are completely incorporated, scraping down the sides and bottom of the bowl as needed. Slowly add the cold water, 1 teaspoon at a time, until you have added 2 teaspoons, scraping down the sides and bottom of the bowl as needed. Stop adding water once the mixture looks shiny—you may not need to use all 3 teaspoons of water. If the almond paste was on the dry side before mixing, you will probably need to add the remaining teaspoon of water. Transfer the finished batter to an airtight container and refrigerate overnight.

3. Preheat the oven to 350°. Line a baking sheet with parchment paper. Fit a piping bag with a ³/₄-inch, number 9, stainless steel round tip and fill the bag with the macaroon batter. Pipe the batter into slightly rounded disks, about 1¹/₄ to 1¹/₂ inches in diameter, onto the parchment-lined baking sheet, 1 inch apart. Dab the center of each disc with a damp paper towel to flatten any peak.

4. Bake for 13 to 15 minutes or until set on the sides—the edges should be light brown and the surfaces lightly crinkled with small, fine cracks. Remove the baking sheet to a wire rack and let the macaroons cool completely on the baking sheet. Gently remove from the paper backing. You can also cut between the rows of cookies with scissors and store them with their paper backing. The macaroons can be kept in an airtight container at room temperature up to 5 days.

For coffee macaroons: Mix together ¼ teaspoon hot water and 1 tablespoon espresso powder until dissolved. In step 2, before refrigerating the batter, whisk the coffee mixture into one-third of the batter until thoroughly mixed. Continue with step 3.

For chocolate macaroons: Before refrigerating the batter in step 2, whisk 2 tablespoons sifted unsweetened cocoa powder into one-third of the batter until thoroughly mixed. Continue with step 3.

MACARONS DE PARIS
Parisian Macaroons

They're called "Macarons" in Paris, but these small almond cookies sandwiched around a variety of flavored fill-ings are more like almond meringues—crunchy on the outside and soft inside. They're often made with almond paste, but we prefer the texture and flavor of finely ground almonds. Use sliced, blanched almonds finely ground in small batches in a coffee grinder. Pipe them carefully: because they're sandwiched together, they should all be the same size. At the bakery, we make many flavors, including pistachio, hazelnut, apple tatin, cognac, passion fruit, cassis, chocolate, raspberry, and lavender. You can have a lot of fun playing with different cookie and filling flavors. Tinted in pastel shades with food coloring, these make nice Easter cookies, and because they're made without flour, they're suitable for Passover, too. Eat them as is or choose a filling or two to fill them with (see Variations).

1. Preheat the oven to 350°. Sift together the powdered sugar and ground almonds into a bowl. In the bowl of an electric mixer fitted with the whisk attachment, whip the egg whites with the salt on medium speed until foamy. Increase the speed to high and gradually add the granulated sugar. Continue to whip to stiff peaks—the whites should be firm and shiny. With a flexible spatula, gently fold in the powdered sugar mixture until completely incorporated.

2. Line baking sheets with parchment paper. Fit a piping bag with a ³⁄₈-inch, number 4, stainless steel round tip and fill the bag with the macaroon batter. Pipe batter into 1-inch disks onto the parchment-lined baking sheet, 2 inches apart. The batter will spread a little; this is nor-mal. Let them dry at room temperature for 15 minutes, or until a soft skin forms on the top of the macaroons and the shiny surface turns dull.

3. Bake, with the door of the oven slightly ajar, for 15 minutes or until the surface of the macaroons is completely dry. Remove baking sheet to a wire rack and let the macaroons cool completely on the baking sheet before gently peeling them off the parchment. The tops are easily crushed, so take care when removing them from the parchment. In an airtight container, the macaroons can be refrigerated up to 2 days or frozen up to 1 month.

4. When filling the macaroons, fill a pastry bag with the desired prepared filling (see Variations). Turn over all the macaroons so their flat bottoms face up. On half of them, pipe out about 1 teaspoon filling and sandwich them with the remaining macaroons, flat-sides down, pressing on them slightly to spread the filling to the edges.

1¼ cups plus 1 teaspoon powdered sugar

4 ounces (1 cup) finely ground, sliced, blanched almonds

¼ cup plus 2 tablespoons fresh egg whites (about 3 extra-large egg whites)

Pinch of salt

¼ cup granulated sugar

MAKES ABOUT SIXTEEN FILLED MACAROONS

BUTTERCREAM

3 egg whites

1 cup sugar

8 ounces (1 cup) unsalted butter, at
room temperature, cut into slices

BUTTERCREAM FOR VARIATIONS

1. In the bowl of an electric mixer, whisk together the egg whites and sugar. Set mixer bowl over a pot of simmering water and heat the mixture, whisking often, until it feels warm to the touch and the sugar is dissolved, 3 to 5 minutes.

2. Transfer the bowl to the electric mixer and fit with the whisk attachment. Whip warm egg mixture on high speed until stiff and shiny, 3 to 5 minutes. Add the butter, one slice at a time, and continue mixing until all the butter is thoroughly incorporated. The buttercream can be kept, covered and refrigerated, up to 1 week. Bring to room temperature before stirring and proceeding. Makes 3 cups.

VARIATIONS

Chocolate: Make the Chocolate Ganache (page 104) using ½ cup heavy cream, 3 ounces bittersweet chocolate and 1 teaspoon light corn syrup. Set aside. In step 1, sift 2 tablespoons unsweetened cocoa powder with the ground almonds and powdered sugar. In step 4, use the ganache for filling.

Raspberry: In step 1, add 2 drops red food coloring to the egg whites after they are whipped. In step 4, use ⅓ cup good-quality raspberry jam for filling.

Cassis (black currant): In step 1, add 2 drops purple food coloring to the egg whites after they are whipped. In step 4, use ⅓ cup good-quality cassis jam for filling.

Hazelnut: In step 1, substitute ½ cup (2 ounces) finely ground, toasted hazelnuts for the ground almonds. In step 4, blend ⅓ cup buttercream (recipe above) with ⅓ cup finely ground hazelnuts for the filling. If desired, add ½ teaspoon hazelnut extract to the filling.

Coffee: In step 1, sift 1 teaspoon freshly ground coffee beans with the ground almonds and powdered sugar. In step 4, blend ⅓ cup buttercream (recipe above) with 2 teaspoons espresso powder for the filling.

Lavender-Honey: In step 1, add 2 teaspoons finely ground (using a coffee grinder) lavender flowers to the sifted almond–powdered sugar mixture. In step 4, blend ⅓ cup buttercream (recipe above) with 2 tablespoons good-quality honey for the filling.

Butter Caramel: In step 3, sprinkle finely chopped toasted hazelnuts on top of macaroon batter before baking. In step 4, use ⅓ cup Butter Caramel (page 128) for filling.

Pistachio: In step 1, add 2 drops green food coloring to the egg whites after they are whipped. In step 4, use ⅓ cup pistachio paste for filling.

BÛCHE DE NOËL AU CHOCOLAT

Chocolate Yule Log

In France, at Christmastime, even the traditional bread bakeries make this famous Yule log. Usually, it's made jelly-roll style, with génoise cake rolled around a buttercream filling and more buttercream "bark" on the outside. Our version is a lot lighter because it's basically a molded mousse with a layer of Chocolate Génoise on the bottom and a dark chocolate ganache glaze. The fun of making a bûche *is in the decorating. A trip to a good baking supplies store during the holidays can provide you everything you need—plastic elves, little wrapped gifts and tiny ornaments. If you're feeling ambitious and you're really in the holiday mood, try making tiny meringue mushrooms, spun-sugar "moss," or chocolate holly leaves with red candy berries. Or simplest of all, just give your* bûche *a light dusting of powdered sugar snow.*

1. Spray a 20 x 3 x 2-inch *Bûche de Noël* mold with vegetable oil spray and line with parchment paper—let the paper overhang the sides by 2 inches. Tape the paper overhang to the outsides of the mold and set aside.

2. To make the Chocolate Génoise: Preheat the oven to 350°. Spray a 12 x 18 x 1-inch baking sheet with vegetable oil spray and line the bottom with parchment paper. Melt the butter and chocolate in a large bowl set over a pot of simmering water, stirring occasionally. Remove from the heat and set aside. In a small bowl, sift together the flour and cocoa powder; set aside. In the bowl of an electric mixer, whisk together the eggs and sugar. Place the mixer bowl over the pot of simmering water and heat the egg mixture, whisking often, until the sugar has dissolved and the eggs feel warm to the touch, 3 to 5 minutes. Transfer the bowl to the electric mixer and fit with the whisk attachment. Whip on high speed until the egg mixture triples in volume, turns pale yellow, and forms thick ribbons when you lift the whisk from the mixture, 3 to 5 minutes. Remove the bowl from the mixer and, using a large flexible spatula, gently but quickly fold the flour mixture into the egg mixture in two additions. Add the melted chocolate and gently fold until combined. Transfer the batter to the prepared baking sheet and, using a spatula, gently ease the batter to the pan edges and smooth the surface with the spatula. Bake the génoise, in the middle of the oven, until the cake springs back when lightly touched, about 12 minutes. Let the cake cool completely in the pan, on a wire rack. To remove the génoise from the pan, run a knife around the pan's perimeter, then place a piece of parchment paper on the surface of the génoise and cover with an inverted cookie sheet. Firmly grasp the edges of both pans, flip the pans over, remove the top pan, and then carefully peel off the parchment paper. Cut the cake into two 3 x 10-inch rectangles and set aside.

CHOCOLATE GÉNOISE

3 ounces (6 tablespoons) unsalted butter

¹/₂ ounce semisweet chocolate, finely chopped (1 tablespoon plus 2 teaspoons)

1¹/₃ cups all-purpose flour

¹/₄ cup unsweetened cocoa powder

6 extra-large eggs

³/₄ cup plus 2 tablespoons sugar

PLAIN CAKE SYRUP

¹/₂ cup water

¹/₂ cup sugar

CHOCOLATE MOUSSE

12 ounces semisweet chocolate, finely chopped (approximately 2 cups)

10 ounces bittersweet chocolate, finely chopped (approximately 1²/₃ cups)

2 cups heavy cream

3 extra-large eggs, separated

Pinch of salt

¹/₄ cup sugar

CHOCOLATE GANACHE

1 cup plus 2 tablespoons heavy cream

4 ounces semisweet chocolate, coarsely chopped (approximately ³/₄ cup)

4 ounces bittersweet chocolate, coarsely chopped (approximately ³/₄ cup)

1 tablespoon light corn syrup

MAKES TWO BÛCHES DE NOËL

3. To make the cake syrup: In a small saucepan, combine the water and sugar and bring to a boil. Remove from heat and set aside to cool.

4. To make the mousse: Melt the semisweet chocolate, bittersweet chocolate, and ¹/₂ cup of the cream in a large bowl, set over a pot of simmering water, stirring occasionally with a flexible spatula. When the chocolate is melted, remove from heat, and whisk in the 3 egg yolks. Set aside. In an electric mixer fitted with the whisk attachment, whip the egg whites and salt on medium speed until foamy. Increase the speed to high and gradually add the sugar. Continue to whip to medium peaks—the peaks will not stand up straight but will droop slightly. In another bowl, whip the remaining 1¹/₂ cups cream to medium peaks. Using a large flexible spatula, fold one-half of the egg whites into the chocolate mixture, and then fold in one-half of the whipped cream. Repeat with the remaining egg whites and whipped cream. Scrape the finished mousse into the prepared *Bûche de Noël* mold and level with a spatula.

5. Brush the génoise pieces with the cake syrup to thoroughly moisten. Flip the pieces over, so the moistened sides are down, and gently place the two pieces, end to end, on top of the mousse. Brush the exposed surface of the génoise generously with syrup. Cover with plastic wrap, lightly pressing down on the cake layers to level, and place in the freezer for 8 hours or until frozen solid.

6. No more than 30 minutes before glazing with chocolate ganache, transfer the frozen *bûche* to the refrigerator. (Timing is important here as the glazing needs to be done while the *bûche* is still frozen.) While the *bûche* is in the refrigerator, make the ganache: In a small saucepan, bring the cream to the scalding point over medium-high heat. In a medium heat-resistant bowl, combine the semisweet chocolate, bittersweet chocolate, and corn syrup. Pour the scalded cream over the chocolate mixture and gently whisk until the chocolate is completely melted and smooth. Remove the *bûche* from the refrigerator. To unmold, release the tape and gently pull up on the parchment paper to release the cake from the mold. Put the *bûche*, cake-side down, on a work surface and, using a knife dipped in hot water, cut into two equal 10-inch-long logs. To glaze the *bûche*, place them on a wire cooling rack set over a baking sheet with raised sides. Rapidly pour the warm glaze evenly over each log. Tap the rack to remove the excess glaze. (The glaze collected on the baking sheet can be saved and reused for attaching decorations.) Using a wide, offset spatula, carefully transfer the glazed *bûche* to a serving platter and decorate as you choose. Store decorated *bûche* in the refrigerator until ready to serve, up to 3 days. Serve slightly chilled.

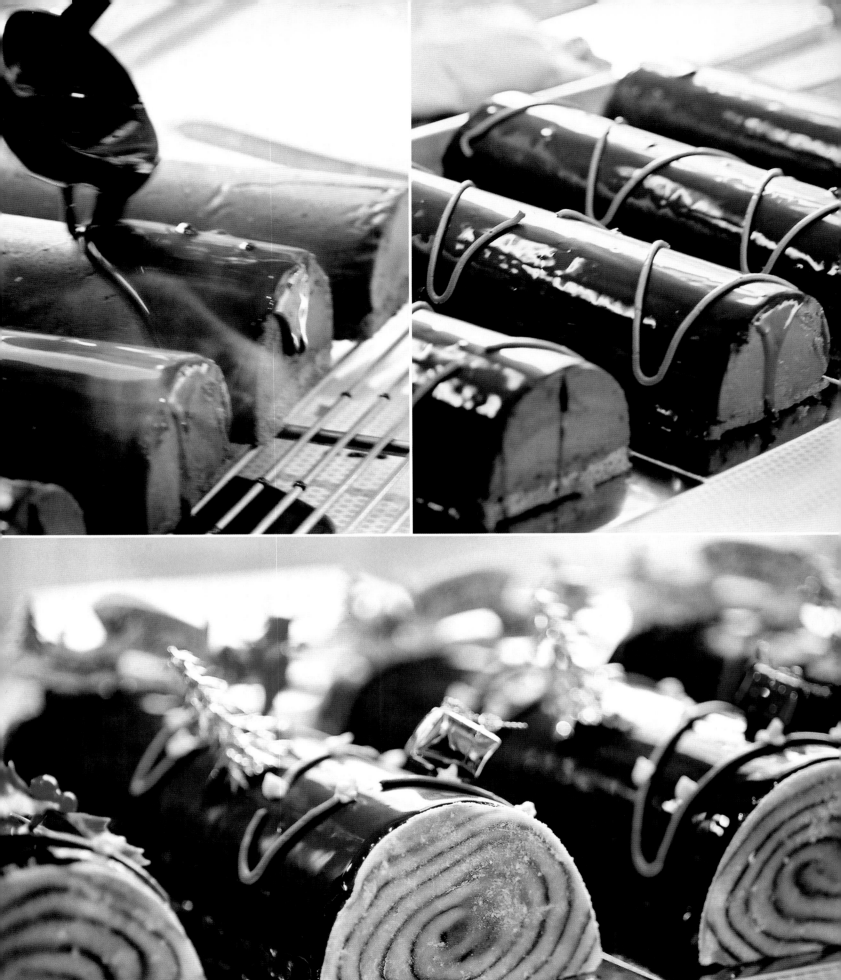

BÛCHE DE NOËL AU CITRON
Lemon Yule Log

One of our pastry chefs at Bay Bread created this alternative to the dark chocolate Bûche de Noël *(page 103)—a rich lemon mousse coated in a white chocolate glaze. Note that the* bûche *needs to be frozen overnight (or for up to two weeks) before glazing, making it a great dessert to do ahead of time.*

1. To make the lemon génoise: Preheat the oven to 350°. Spray a 12 x 18 x 1-inch baking sheet with vegetable oil spray and line the bottom with parchment paper. In the bowl of an electric mixer, whisk together the eggs and sugar. Place the mixer bowl over a pot of simmering water and heat the egg mixture, whisking often, until the sugar has dissolved and the eggs feel warm to the touch, 3 to 5 minutes. Transfer the bowl to the electric mixer and fit with the whisk attachment. Add the lemon zest. Whip on high speed until the egg mixture triples in volume, turns pale yellow, and forms thick ribbons when you lift the whisk from the mixture, 3 to 5 minutes. Remove the bowl from the mixer and, using a large flexible spatula, gently but quickly fold the flour into the egg mixture. When the flour is almost completely incorporated, add the melted butter and fold just until combined. Transfer the batter to the prepared baking sheet and, using a spatula, gently ease the batter to the pan edges and smooth the surface. Bake the génoise, in the middle of the oven, until the cake is lightly browned and springs back when lightly touched, about 12 minutes. Let the cake cool completely in the pan, on a wire rack. To remove the génoise from the pan, run a knife around the pan's edges, then place a piece of parchment paper on the surface of the génoise and cover with an inverted cookie sheet. Firmly grasp the edges of both pans, flip the pans over, remove the top pan, and then carefully peel off the parchment paper. Cut the cake into two 3 x 10-inch rectangles and set aside.

2. Spray a 20 x 3 x 2-inch *Bûche de Noël* mold with vegetable oil spray and line with parchment paper—let the paper overhang the sides by 2 inches. Tape the paper overhang to the outsides of the mold and set aside.

3. To make the cake syrup: In a small saucepan, combine the water and sugar and bring to a boil. Remove from the heat, stir in the strained lemon juice, and set aside to cool.

4. To make the mousse: In the bowl of an electric mixer fitted with the paddle attachment, beat the cream cheese on medium speed until light and fluffy, scraping down the sides and bottom of the bowl as needed. Reduce the speed to low, add the sugar, then increase the speed to medium and beat until light and fluffy. Reduce the speed to low, add the lemon juice and lemon zest, and mix until smooth. Remove the bowl

LEMON GÉNOISE

6 eggs

1 cup sugar

2 teaspoons freshly grated lemon zest

1¹/₂ cups all-purpose flour, sifted

4 ounces (¹/₂ cup) unsalted butter, melted

CAKE SYRUP

¹/₂ cup water

¹/₂ cup sugar

¹/₄ cup fresh lemon juice, strained

LEMON MOUSSE

12 ounces cream cheese, at room temperature

³/₄ cup plus 2 tablespoons sugar

¹/₄ cup fresh lemon juice, strained

1 tablespoon freshly grated lemon zest

3 sheets gelatin, softened in water, drained and set aside (see sidebar)

2 cups heavy cream, whipped to medium peaks and refrigerated

WHITE CHOCOLATE GLAZE

14 ounces white chocolate, finely chopped (approximately 2¹/₂ cups)

1 cup heavy cream

4¹/₂ ounces (9 tablespoons) unsalted butter, at room temperature

MAKES TWO BÛCHES DE NOËL

Gelatin has the ability to turn a liquid into a solid, a process that involves softening, heating, and chilling. Gelatin for culinary use is made from pigs' skin, and is therefore not kosher. Kosher brands are, however, available.

Unflavored gelatin is available in two forms: powdered and sheet—often called "leaf" gelatin. One level teaspoon of powdered gelatin equals 3 grams. The powder must be sprinkled over a specified amount of cold water in a bowl and left to soften for a few minutes. Once softened, the gelatin must be heated to completely dissolve. See the back of the gelatin package or box for specific details. (1 teaspoon powdered gelatin should be sprinkled over 4 teaspoons cold water.)

One sheet, or leaf, of gelatin equals 3 grams. To soften gelatin sheets, submerge them in a bowl of cold water and let soften for about 5 minutes or so. The sheet will be completely soft, with no dry pieces. Once softened, gently squeeze out the excess water and then heat to dissolve.

from the mixer. Dissolve softened gelatin in a small saucepan over low heat. Stir 1 cup of the cream cheese mixture into the dissolved gelatin, then fold the gelatin mixture into the remaining cream cheese mixture. Finish the mousse by quickly folding in the whipped cream until combined. Scrape the finished mousse into the prepared *Bûche de Noël* mold and level with a spatula.

5. Brush the lemon génoise pieces with cake syrup to thoroughly moisten. Flip the pieces over, so the moistened sides are down, and gently place the two pieces, end to end, on top of the mousse. Brush the exposed surface of the génoise generously with syrup. Cover with plastic wrap, lightly pressing down on the cake layers to level, and place in the freezer for 8 hours or until frozen solid.

6. No more than 30 minutes before glazing, transfer the *bûche* to the refrigerator. (Timing is important here, as the glazing needs to be done while the *bûche* is still frozen.) While the *bûche* is in the refrigerator, make the glaze: Place the white chocolate in a heat-resistant bowl. In a saucepan, bring the cream just to the boiling point over medium-high heat. Pour the hot cream over the chocolate and whisk until the chocolate is completely melted and smooth. Slowly whisk in the soft butter, a tablespoon at a time, until incorporated.

7. Remove the *bûche* from the refrigerator. To unmold, release the tape and gently pull up on the parchment paper to release the cake from the mold. Put the *bûche*, cake-side down, on a work surface and, using a knife dipped in hot water, cut into two equal 10-inch-long logs. To glaze the *bûche*, place them on a cooling rack set over a baking sheet with raised sides. Rapidly pour the warm glaze evenly over each log. Tap the rack to remove the excess glaze. (The glaze collected on the baking sheet can be saved and reused for attaching decorations.) Using a wide, offset spatula, carefully transfer the glazed *bûche* to a serving platter and decorate as you choose. Store decorated *bûche* in the refrigerator until ready to serve, up to 3 days. Serve slightly chilled.

MARQUISE AU CHOCOLAT

Chocolate Marquise

Seventy years ago, the chocolate marquise cake, which took the improbable form of a beautiful noblewoman with a billowing polka-dotted hoopskirt—was all the rage in France. I had a hunch that San Francisco might just be the perfect place to revive this curious confection, but everyone at the bakery rolled their eyes and told me I was nuts. All the same, I started calling baking suppliers in France, just to see if I could find the molds. Eventually, I hooked up with a fellow who still had twenty molds left over from the 1930s, and I took that as a good omen. We perfected our version of the marquise cake, and sure enough, it was an instant succés fou. Within the first year we sold more than 300 of them!

1. To make the vanilla génoise: Preheat the oven to 350°. Spray a 12 x 18 x 1-inch baking sheet with vegetable oil spray and line the bottom with parchment paper. In the bowl of an electric mixer, whisk together the eggs and sugar. Place the mixer bowl over a pot of simmering water and heat the egg mixture, whisking often, until the sugar has dissolved and the eggs feel warm to the touch, 3 to 5 minutes. Transfer the bowl to the electric mixer and fit with the whisk attachment. Add the vanilla bean scrapings (save the pod for another use). Whip on high speed until the egg mixture triples in volume, turns pale yellow, and forms thick ribbons when you lift the whisk from the mixture, 3 to 5 minutes. Remove the bowl from the mixer and, using a large flexible spatula, gently but quickly fold the flour into the egg mixture. When the flour is almost completely incorporated, add the melted butter and fold just until combined. Transfer the batter to the prepared baking sheet and gently smooth the surface with a spatula. Bake the génoise, in the middle of the oven, until the cake is lightly browned and springs back when lightly touched, about 12 minutes. Let the cake cool completely in the pan, on a wire rack. To remove the génoise from the pan, run a knife around the pan's perimeter, then place a piece of parchment paper on the surface of the génoise and cover with an inverted cookie sheet. Firmly grasp the edges of both pans, flip the pans over, remove the top pan, and then carefully peel off the parchment paper.

2. To assemble the marquise: Place one-half of the chocolate mousse in the bottom of a 1½-quart metal mixing bowl. Measure the diameter of the bowl at the level of the mousse's surface, and cut a round from the génoise that is 1-inch smaller in diameter. (The cake should not touch the sides of the bowl.) Place the cake round directly on the surface of the mousse and, using a pastry brush, soak the génoise with the cake syrup. Top the cake with the remaining chocolate mousse, filling the bowl to within ¾ inch of the rim. Again, measure the diameter of the bowl at the level of the mousse's surface, and cut a round from the génoise,

VANILLA GÉNOISE

6 extra-large eggs

1 cup sugar

1 vanilla bean, split lengthwise and scraped

1½ cups all-purpose flour, sifted

4 ounces (½ cup) unsalted butter, melted

1 recipe Chocolate Mousse (page 103)

1 recipe Plain Cake Syrup (page 103)

1 recipe Chocolate Ganache (page 104)

1 plastic marquise doll, for decoration

Approximately 15 Macarons de Paris (page 101), for decoration

MAKES ONE CHOCOLATE MARQUISE

1-inch smaller in diameter. (The remaining génoise may be frozen, wrapped tightly in plastic, for use at a later date.) Place the cake round directly on the surface of the mousse and, using a pastry brush, soak the génoise with the cake syrup. Press the génoise down gently so it is flush with the rim of the bowl and the mousse rises up the sides of the bowl, level with the cake. Place a piece of plastic wrap directly on the surface of the soaked génoise and freeze for at least 6 hours.

3. To glaze the *Marquise:* Place the chocolate ganache in a large, heat-resistant bowl set over a pot of simmering water, and heat, stirring occasionally, until liquid—it should be warm but not hot. Meanwhile, dip the frozen marquise in a bowl of very hot water for just a few seconds, to melt the outermost layer of mousse. Immediately invert the marquise onto a wire rack set over a baking sheet with raised sides. (If further coaxing is necessary to unmold the marquise, firmly grab both the inverted bowl and the rack and shake gently to release.) To glaze the cake, rapidly pour the warm ganache evenly over the cake. Tap the rack to remove the excess glaze. (The glaze collected on the baking sheet can be saved and reused to attach the macaroons for decoration.) Gently insert the top half of the doll into the top of the cake. Using a wide, offset metal spatula, carefully transfer the marquise to an 8-inch cardboard cake circle or platter and refrigerate until the ganache is set, about 30 minutes. The marquise may be served at this point or further adorned as follows.

4. Place the collected chocolate ganache drippings in a large, heat-resistant bowl set over a pan of simmering water. Heat, stirring occasionally, until soft but not liquid. Remove the marquise from the refrigerator and, using the soft ganache as "glue," affix the macaroons around the "skirt's" circumference, working from the bottom to the top, finishing the bottom row before starting the next row. The marquise can be refrigerated up to 24 hours, but should be removed from the refrigerator 30 minutes before serving. To serve, bring the marquise to the table in all her splendor.

LA PÂTISSERIE RUSTIQUE
Country-Style Pastries

In France, the kinds of baked goods you find in the display case of a boulangerie depend on where the shop is and what kind of customers it caters to. Of course, there is bread. Then, in order of sophistication, you might find some *pâtisserie rustique*, and some *specialités*. That middle category of *pâtisserie rustique*, which is all the simple tarts and cakes, is quite common because those items are easy for the *boulanger* to produce—and also very easy to sell, since everyone loves them.

This is really home-style baking, and I think you will have fun with the *pâtisserie* in this chapter, because they don't require a lot of complicated or time-consuming techniques. In recipes like these, "rustic" doesn't mean "crude," it means honest, straightforward, and without any kind of tricks or artifice to get in the way of the flavors. With that kind of simplicity, you have nowhere to hide. You have to use really good ingredients, like fresh, ripe, locally grown fruit from a farmers' market, the best chocolate, and high-quality dairy products. Stick to that idea and you will experience the infinite pleasures of simple French baking—and pastry that is every bit as astonishing as the fancy stuff.

PÂTE SUCRÉE
Sweet Tart Dough

This is the classic, flaky pastry dough used to make many of the tarts in this chapter. Depending on the filling, it can be prebaked before filling, or simply rolled out, pressed into the pan, refrigerated until firm, and then filled and baked (as for rustic-style tarts in this chapter, which are made in a deep springform pan). It's rich and sweet, like a butter-cookie dough, and can, in fact, be used to make very nice sablé-style cookies, simply by rolling it out, cutting it into shapes, and sprinkling them with a bit of unrefined coarse brown sugar. Don't be put off by the dough's soft texture, which can make it a little tricky to handle. That softness comes from the butter and powdered sugar, and those are the secrets that make it so rich and flavorful. Try not to overwork the dough, which will cause it to toughen and shrink in the pan when baked.

4^1/$_2$ ounces (9 tablespoons) unsalted butter, at room temperature

1 cup plus 3 tablespoons powdered sugar

^{1}/$_2$ teaspoon salt

2^3/$_4$ cups all-purpose flour

2 extra-large eggs, well beaten

MAKES TWO 9-INCH RUSTIC TART SHELLS OR TWO 9-INCH TART SHELLS

1. In the bowl of an electric mixer fitted with the paddle attachment, cream the butter, powdered sugar, and salt on low speed. Gradually add the flour and mix until a sandy texture forms. Add the eggs in a steady stream and mix until a smooth dough forms. Divide the dough into two equal pieces. Flatten each piece of dough into a disk about ^{1}/$_2$-inch thick, wrap each in plastic, and refrigerate until firm, at least 30 minutes. (If only making one tart, the extra dough may be refrigerated up to 3 days or frozen up to 1 month.)

2. With vegetable oil spray, lightly coat two shallow (1-inch sides) 9-inch diameter tart pans with removable bottoms, or a deep (2-inch sides) 9-inch diameter springform pan with removable bottom. Transfer the chilled dough to a lightly floured work surface and, using a rolling pin, flatten it between two sheets of plastic wrap to form a circle 12^1/$_2$ inches in diameter and ^{1}/$_4$-inch thick. Remove the top sheet of plastic wrap, flip the dough over, and ease it into the prepared pan. Remove the remaining sheet of plastic wrap, and press the dough gently into the edges of the pan. Trim the edge by running your rolling pin over the top of the pan. Repeat process with remaining dough. Wrap tart pans tightly in plastic wrap and refrigerate until firm.

3. For rustic tart shells in the springform pans, wrap tightly in plastic wrap and refrigerate for up to 3 days or freeze for up to 1 month. (Rustic tart shells are not prebaked.)

4. To prebake the shallow 9-inch-diameter tart shell, preheat the oven to 375°. Bake for 15 to 20 minutes or until golden brown.

CRÈME PÂTISSIÈRE
Pastry Cream

We use this rich custard filling as a basic "building block" in a number of recipes. While a classic Crème Pâtissière *would typically be made with flour, this one is thickened with cornstarch, which gives it a silkier texture and an attractive sheen. You can use it to make a simple fruit tart. Once it has chilled, just spread it into a prebaked* Pâte Sucrée *shell (page 114) and top with fresh berries or other ripe fruit. If desired, brush the top with a glaze of warm, strained apricot preserves. Or simpler still, just enjoy* Crème Pâtissière *warm or chilled as a pudding, topped with crumbled cookies.*

1. In a medium saucepan, bring 3 cups of the milk to a boil over high heat. Meanwhile, in a medium bowl, whisk together the sugar and cornstarch. In a small bowl, whisk together the eggs, egg yolks, and remaining cup of milk. Add the egg mixture to the sugar mixture and whisk until smooth. Once the milk comes to a boil, gently pour half of the hot milk into the egg mixture, whisking constantly. Return the saucepan to the heat and whisk the tempered egg mixture into the milk remaining in the saucepan. Cook, whisking constantly to make sure the bottom doesn't scorch, until the pastry cream thickens and bubbles erupt on the surface, 5 to 10 minutes. Remove from the heat and stir in the vanilla. Transfer to a small bowl and place a piece of plastic wrap directly on the surface of the pastry cream. Pastry cream can be kept, covered and refrigerated, up to 4 days.

4 cups whole milk

1 cup sugar

$^1/_2$ cup cornstarch

2 extra-large eggs, at room temperature

2 extra-large egg yolks, at room temperature

1 tablespoon vanilla extract

MAKES 4$^1/_2$ CUPS PASTRY CREAM

FLAN PÂTISSIER aux CERISES

Baked Cherry Flan

This might just be my favorite of all the things we make at our boulangerie because it's my "Madeleine de Proust." It was my after-school snack almost every day when I was growing up, and for me, part of the Proustian experience is the hint of metallic flavor from the iron pan. I always loved the crusty, caramelized bits around the edge the most. I've noticed that this tart, with its soft texture and intentionally soggy crust is downright strange to most Americans, who tend to think of flan as being more like crème caramel or custard. But it's extremely popular in France, and for me it's the kind of perfect comfort food I could eat forever, until I'm old and toothless.

8 ounces chilled Puff Pastry Dough (page 38)

2 cups whole milk

1/2 cup sugar

1/4 cup cornstarch

1 extra-large egg, at room temperature

1 extra-large egg yolk, at room temperature

1 1/2 teaspoons vanilla extract

1/2 cup dried or fresh cherries, pitted

MAKES ONE 9-INCH TART

1. With vegetable oil spray, lightly coat a shallow 9-inch-diameter tart pan with removable bottom. On a lightly floured work surface, roll out the puff pastry dough into a 12-inch circle about 1/4-inch thick. Ease the dough into the prepared pan, pressing the dough gently into the edges of the pan. Leave the excess dough hanging over the side of the pan. Wrap in plastic wrap and freeze until firm, 10 to 15 minutes. When it is chilled, trim the excess dough by running a rolling pin or pressing a metal spatula over the edge of the pan. Using a fork, lightly prick the bottom of the tart. Wrap in plastic wrap and refrigerate until ready to fill.

2. To make the filling: In a medium saucepan, bring 1 1/2 cups of the milk to a boil over high heat. Meanwhile, in a medium bowl, whisk together the sugar and cornstarch. In a small bowl, whisk together the egg, egg yolk, and remaining 1/2 cup milk. Combine the egg and sugar mixture and whisk until smooth. Once the milk comes to a boil, pour half of the hot milk into the egg mixture, whisking constantly. Return this to the saucepan on the heat and whisk. Cook, whisking constantly to make sure the bottom doesn't scorch, until the pastry cream thickens and bubbles erupt on the surface, 5 to 10 minutes. Stir in the vanilla extract. Transfer the pastry cream to a small bowl and place a piece of plastic wrap directly on the surface. Let sit 30 minutes at room temperature before proceeding. Do not refrigerate or the finished tart will have large cracks.

3. Position the oven rack in the top third of the oven and preheat the oven to 425°. Spread approximately half of the warm pastry cream in the bottom of the tart shell. Sprinkle the cherries over the top of the pastry cream, then cover the cherries with the remaining pastry cream. Using a large metal spatula, smooth and level the pastry cream even with the top edge of the pan. Place on a parchment paper–lined baking sheet and bake for 30 minutes or until the filling is puffed and the top is spotted brown. Transfer the baking sheet to a wire rack and let the flan cool to room temperature. Chill the flan, uncovered, in the refrigerator, preferably overnight, before removing the sides from the pan and cutting. The flan is always served cold. The flan can be stored in the refrigerator up to 3 days.

TARTE RUSTIQUE aux POMMES
Rustic Apple Tart

What I love about this tart is that it's all about the apples. There's no pastry cream or fancy ingredients to get in the way, so what you experience is the blend of great Pâte Sucrée and perfectly cooked apples that is just so right and true. It's not overly sweetened, so the apple flavor can come through. We use Granny Smiths for their tanginess. And please, leave the cinnamon in the cupboard for this one.

1. Preheat the oven to 425°. Using a fork, lightly prick the bottom of the tart shell and refrigerate until ready to fill.

2. To make apple filling: Peel, core, and halve the apples. With flat sides down, slice crosswise into ⅛-inch slices; transfer to a large bowl and toss with the lemon juice. Set aside one-third of the apple slices for decorating the top of the tart. Using your hands, toss the remaining apple slices with the flour and sugar. Transfer to the cold tart shell, patting the apples level.

3. Using the reserved apple slices, form a spiral design over the apple filling: start in the center of the tart and work out to the edge of the pan, overlapping the apple slices by about one-half the width of the slices. The rows should overlap as well, as the apples will shrink during baking. Sprinkle the top of the tart with ¼ cup of sugar and dot with the cold butter slices.

4. Bake in the center of the oven for 25 minutes, then lower the temperature to 350° and bake for 45 minutes longer, or until well browned and the juices are bubbling. Cool on a wire rack before removing the sides from the pan. Serve at room temperature, or even cold. To store, cover with plastic wrap and refrigerate up to 3 days.

1 chilled, unbaked deep 9-inch Pâte Sucrée rustic tart shell (page 114)

APPLE FILLING

7 medium (about 3¼ pounds) Granny Smith apples

2 teaspoons fresh lemon juice

2 tablespoons all-purpose flour

¼ cup sugar

TART TOPPING

¼ cup sugar

2 ounces (4 tablespoons) cold unsalted butter, sliced

MAKES ONE 9-INCH TART

TARTE RUSTIQUE AUX POIRES

Rustic Pear Streusel Tart

My grandmother had a pear tree, and although I have no idea what kind of pears it produced, I remember that they were unbelievable—grainy and intensely delicious. She used those pears to make wonderful fruit tarts like this one (minus the streusel). I like the little bit of extra crunch the streusel adds and the way it contrasts with the juicy fruit and the soft sweet tart dough. I recommend using pears that are ripe but still quite firm, and leaving the peel on to help the slices hold their shape. At the Boulangerie we have also made this tart with other seasonal fruits, and one of our spring favorites is strawberry-rhubarb (see Variation).

---

1 chilled, unbaked deep 9-inch Pâte Sucrée rustic tart shell (page 114)

PEAR FILLING

7 medium (2 pounds) French Butter pears, ripe but firm

1 teaspoon vanilla extract

1/2 cup sugar

2 tablespoons all-purpose flour

1 tablespoon tapioca flour

STREUSEL TOPPING

3/4 cups plus 2 tablespoons all-purpose flour

1/3 cup firmly packed light brown sugar

3 ounces (1/3 cup) cold, unsalted butter, cut into cubes

MAKES ONE 9-INCH TART

1. Preheat the oven to 425°. Using a fork, lightly prick the bottom of the tart shell and refrigerate until ready to fill.

2. To make the filling: Cut the pears in half (leaving skin on) and, using a melon baller or a small spoon, remove the core. Cut each pear half into 10 lengthwise slices. Place the pear slices in a large bowl and toss with the vanilla extract. Add the sugar, all-purpose flour, and tapioca flour and toss again. Set aside.

3. To make the streusel: In the bowl of an electric mixer fitted with the paddle attachment, combine the all-purpose flour and brown sugar on low speed. Add the butter and continue mixing until fine and crumbly— do not overmix. It's okay if there are some butter chunks remaining.

4. Set aside 7 of the pear slices, then transfer the remaining pear mixture to the cold tart shell, patting to level the fruit. Arrange the reserved pears in a pinwheel design in the center of the tart. Sprinkle the streusel around the outside of the pinwheel.

5. Bake in the center of the 425° oven for 25 minutes, then lower the temperature to 350° and bake for 45 minutes longer, or until well browned and the juices are bubbling. Cool on a wire rack before removing from the pan. Serve at room temperature, or even cold. To store, cover with plastic wrap and refrigerate up to 3 days.

VARIATION

In step 2, substitute 3 cups halved strawberries, 5 cups rhubarb, cut into 1-inch pieces, 1/2 cup sugar, 2 tablespoons all-purpose flour, 2 table-spoons tapioca flour, 1 teaspoon lemon juice, and 1 teaspoon freshly grated orange zest. Continue with recipe from step 3.

TARTE RUSTIQUE aux PRUNES et AUX BAIES
Rustic Plum-Berry Tart

Like the Rustic Apple Tart (page 119), this dessert is a study in simplicity, balance, and restraint. With so few ingredients, what you put in is what you get back, so of course, it's critical that the plums and berries be mouth-wateringly good to begin with. I like to eat this tart as a snack on the run, or warm with vanilla ice cream.

1. Preheat the oven to 425°. Using a fork, lightly prick the bottom of the tart shell and refrigerate until ready to fill.

2. Cut the plums in half, discard the pits, and cut each half into thirds. In a large bowl, combine the plums, lemon juice, sugar, tapioca flour, and all-purpose flour and mix well. Allow to sit for at least 10 minutes or until the plums give up some of their juices. Toss in the berries and mix well. Transfer to the cold tart shell, patting to level the fruit. Flip the plum pieces skin-side down, as the skin can burn during the long cooking.

3. Bake in the center of the oven at 425° for 25 minutes, then lower the temperature to 350° and bake for 45 minutes longer, or until well browned and the juices are bubbling. Cool on a wire rack before removing sides from the pan. Serve at room temperature, or even cold. To store, cover with plastic wrap and refrigerate up to 3 days.

1 chilled, unbaked deep 9-inch Pâte Sucrée rustic tart shell (page 114)

PLUM-BERRY FILLING

8 to 12 medium (about 2 pounds) Mariposa or other variety plums

2 teaspoons fresh lemon juice

1/2 cup sugar

3 tablespoons tapioca flour

2 tablespoons all-purpose flour

1 cup fresh berries (raspberries, blackberries, and/or strawberries)

MAKES ONE 9-INCH TART

TARTE TATIN
Caramelized Apple Tart

Some people say this upside-down apple tart was invented by the Tatin sisters, who ran an inn in the Loire Valley. The story goes that they dropped an apple tart on the kitchen table and when it landed upside down, they decided to bake and serve it just like that. That was a happy accident, because the inverted baking technique that is now standard practice for this famous tart makes everything turn out perfectly: The apples caramelize in the hot pan, and the pastry, which is exposed during baking, becomes light and flaky. Because the crust doesn't really need to rise very high, this is an excellent way to use up leftover puff pastry trimmings.

CARAMEL

1 ounce (2 tablespoons) unsalted butter

2 cups sugar

APPLES

8 medium (about 3³/₄ pounds) Granny Smith apples, peeled

8 ounces Puff Pastry Dough (page 38)

MAKES ONE 10-INCH TART

1. To make the caramel: Have ready a 10-inch-diameter round cake pan with 3-inch sides. (Do not use a springform pan for this; it will leak!) In a medium saucepan, melt the butter over medium heat. Add the sugar and cook, stirring often with a wooden spoon, until the mixture is dark amber in color—it's okay if there are a few sugar lumps remaining. When the caramel is done, carefully pour it into the cake pan. Don't touch the cake pan with unprotected hands—it will be hot! Set the cake pan aside until caramel is cool. (The caramel-coated pan can be made up to 2 days in advance and left, covered, at room temperature.)

2. Preheat the oven to 400°. Core the apples by cutting down, top to bottom, on all four sides around the core. You will have two apple halves and two smaller pieces. Arrange the first layer of apple halves, flat-side down, on top of the set caramel in the pan. (This will later become the top of the tart.) Arrange the remaining apple halves and pieces to form the second layer. Things will be a bit crowded at first, but the apples will shrink down when cooked. Place on a parchment paper–lined, sturdy baking sheet. Bake for about 50 minutes, until the apples are very tender.

3. Meanwhile, on a lightly floured work surface, roll out the puff pastry dough into a round ¼-inch thick. Cut out a 10-inch pastry circle and transfer it to a parchment-lined baking sheet. Cover with plastic wrap and refrigerate until needed.

4. When apples are done, carefully remove the baking sheet from the oven and transfer to a flat surface, taking care, as the caramel will be bubbling hot. Remove the pastry circle from the refrigerator and prick with a fork 15 times. Gently place on top of the cooked apples. Return tart to the oven and bake for 35 minutes or until the puff pastry is puffy and golden brown. Cool in the pan on a wire rack for 20 to 25 minutes.

5. To serve, you will need a 12- to 14-inch-diameter round serving platter and another sturdy baking sheet. Invert both the serving platter and the other baking sheet over the warm *tatin* pan. Using both hands, firmly grab both baking sheets and quickly flip over the pans—doing this over the kitchen sink will cut down on any sticky mess. Remove the top baking sheet and carefully lift up the cake pan, using dry towels to avoid getting burned by the caramel. If any apples remain stuck to the pan, remove them with a metal spatula and place them back on the tart. This tart is best served warm.

TARTE AU CITRON
Lemon Tart

This is a classic boulangerie recipe, and I think that over the years we have really arrived at the quintessential version. It's creamy and tangy, and it tastes just exactly as it should—like bright, fresh lemons.

1. Place the prebaked tart shell on a parchment paper–lined baking sheet. Set aside. In a medium, stainless steel saucepan, whisk together the eggs, sugar, lemon juice, lemon zest, and cream over low heat. Cook, stirring constantly with a heat-resistant flexible spatula to avoid scorching, until slightly thickened, 8 to 12 minutes. Do not let the custard get so hot that it bubbles, as this will curdle the filling. The filling should lightly coat the spatula when it's done. If not using right away, transfer to a small bowl and place a piece of plastic wrap directly on the surface of the custard. The custard can be kept, covered and refrigerated, up to 5 days. If chilled, bring the filling to room temperature before proceeding.

2. Preheat the oven to 325°. Pour the filling into the tart shell to within ½ inch of the top, and smooth the surface.

3. Bake for 25 to 35 minutes or until just set. To test, gently jostle the baking sheet—the edges will be set but the very center will move softly like a bowl of gelatin. Cool in the pan on a wire rack, and then refrigerate for at least 2 hours to set the tart completely. Just before serving, remove the side of the pan and transfer the tart to a serving platter.

1 prebaked shallow 9-inch Pâte Sucrée tart shell (page 114)

4 extra-large eggs, at room temperature

1 cup sugar

¼ cup plus 2 tablespoons fresh lemon juice, strained

1 tablespoon freshly grated lemon zest

½ cup plus 1 tablespoon heavy cream

MAKES ONE 9-INCH TART

TARTE À LA CITROUILLE ET À LA CRÈME FRAÎCHE
Pumpkin Tart with Crème Fraîche

You won't find this in a traditional boulangerie in France, but we are an American Boulangerie, and every so often we adopt a baking idea or two from our transplanted homeland—like pumpkin pie. This one came from one of our pastry chefs, who got us all hooked on her family's pumpkin tart recipe. She adds a swirl of crème fraîche, which gives it extra richness and makes a nice contrast to the spices. We always use sugar pumpkins, but canned pumpkin (just the pumpkin, not the seasoned pie filling) is almost as tasty.

PUMPKIN FILLING

1¼ cups (10 ounces) solid pack pumpkin purée

½ cup plus 2 tablespoons firmly packed dark brown sugar

1 teaspoon ground cinnamon

½ teaspoon ground ginger

¼ teaspoon ground nutmeg

⅛ teaspoon ground cloves

2 extra-large eggs

1 cup heavy cream

1 chilled, unbaked deep 9-inch Pâte Sucrée rustic tart shell (page 114)

¼ cup crème fraîche, for garnish

MAKES ONE 9-INCH TART

1. Preheat the oven to 350°. To make the filling: In a large bowl, whisk together the pumpkin purée, brown sugar, cinnamon, ginger, nutmeg, and clove. Add the eggs, then whisk in the heavy cream until well combined. Pour the filling into the chilled tart shell. Dollop on the crème fraîche and, using a knife, swirl into an attractive design on top of the pumpkin filling.

2. Bake for 40 to 50 minutes or until the filling is set. Cool completely on a wire rack before removing from pan. The tart is best at room temperature the day it is baked, but it can be kept, covered and refrigerated, up to 3 days.

TARTE AUX TROIS NOIX

Triple-Nut Tart

Like our Pumpkin Tart with Crème Fraîche (page 126), this is an ideal winter dessert to make when good fresh fruit is less available. It, too, is a not-very-French homage to California—and to another American classic, pecan pie. Try serving it (as we don't say in France) à la mode, with vanilla ice cream. We use a mixture of pecans, walnuts, and pine nuts, which give a nice balance, but feel free to go nuts and experiment with your favorites.

1. Preheat the oven to 350°. To make the filling: In a small saucepan, melt the butter over low heat. Reduce heat to medium and continue to cook, swirling the pan occasionally, until the butter is deep brown and smells nutty and delicious. (At first the butter will bubble wildly, and then the solids will start to sink to the bottom of the pan and turn brown.) Be careful not to let it burn; the difference between deep brown and black is a matter of seconds. Remove the pan from the heat. In a medium bowl, whisk together the browned butter, brown sugar, honey, corn syrup, flour, eggs, rum, and salt until smooth. (At this point the filling can be kept in an airtight container in the refrigerator, up to 5 days. Bring to room temperature and stir before proceeding.)

2. Place the tart shell pan on a parchment paper–lined baking sheet. Scatter the toasted nuts in the tart shell, and then pour the filling over the nuts in a zigzag fashion to within 1/2 inch of the top.

3. Bake for 17 to 20 minutes or until golden brown and the filling is puffed and set. Cool on a wire rack before removing from the pan. It is easiest to slice at room temperature.

FILLING

1 1/2 ounces (3 tablespoons) unsalted butter

1/2 cup firmly packed dark brown sugar

1/4 cup honey

3 tablespoons dark corn syrup

1 tablespoon all-purpose flour

3 extra-large eggs, at room temperature

1 tablespoon plus 1 teaspoon dark rum (optional)

Scant 1/4 teaspoon salt

1 cup mixed nuts, toasted

1 prebaked shallow 9-inch Pâte Sucrée tart shell (page 114)

MAKES ONE 9-INCH TART

TARTELETTES au CHOCOLAT, NOIX, et CARAMEL

Chocolate-Caramel-Pecan Tartlets

I like these individual mini-tarts because you don't have to share. With their layers of toasted pecans, buttery caramel, and dark chocolate ganache, they have the rich, gooey, crunchy appeal of those famous "turtle" candies, but with a more intense flavor. We think 3½-inch tartlets are just right, but you can also use this recipe to make a single 9-inch tart.

CHOCOLATE TARTLET DOUGH

6 ounces (³/₄ cup) unsalted butter

1 cup sugar

¹/₄ teaspoon salt

1 cup unsweetened cocoa powder, preferably Dutch-process

2 cups all-purpose flour

³/₄ teaspoon vanilla extract

¹/₄ cup water

BUTTER CARAMEL FILLING

2 cups sugar

3 tablespoons corn syrup

1¹/₂ cups cream

4 ounces (¹/₂ cup) unsalted butter

CHOCOLATE GANACHE

1 cup plus 2 tablespoons heavy cream

4 ounces bittersweet chocolate, coarsely chopped (approximately ³/₄ cup)

4 ounces semisweet chocolate, coarsely chopped (approximately ³/₄ cup)

1 tablespoon light corn syrup

TOPPING

1¹/₂ cups pecans, toasted and chopped

MAKES TEN TARTLETS

1. To make the chocolate tartlet dough: In the bowl of an electric mixer fitted with the paddle attachment, cream the butter, sugar, and salt on medium speed until smooth. Add the cocoa powder and mix on low speed until combined, scraping down the sides and bottom of the bowl as needed. Add the flour and mix until incorporated, stopping once to scrape down the sides and bottom of the bowl. With the mixer still on low speed, add the extract and the water in a steady stream and mix just until incorporated. The batter will not be completely smooth. Turn the dough out onto a work surface, flatten into a disk, and wrap in plastic wrap. Refrigerate the dough for at least 30 minutes. (At this point, the dough can be refrigerated for up to 3 days or frozen up to 1 month.)

2. Arrange ten 3½-inch tartlet pans with removable bottoms on a baking sheet. Spray the pans lightly with vegetable oil spray. Place the chilled dough on a lightly floured work surface and roll into a round approximately ⅛-inch thick. (Lift the dough off the work surface and turn it 90 degrees each time you roll to make sure the dough doesn't stick and is being rolled evenly.) Place an inverted tartlet pan on the rolled dough and, using the pan as a guide, cut a 5½-inch-diameter circle. Cut as many circles of dough as possible and set aside. Gather the remaining scraps of dough and repeat the rolling and cutting process. Fit a circle of dough gently into each pan, making sure that the dough is pressed gently into the bottom edge of each pan. Gently press along the insides of each pan to smooth the dough. Run the rolling pin over the top edges to trim the excess dough off the tartlet shells. Using a fork, prick the bottom of each tartlet shell to prevent air bubbles from forming when baking. Transfer the tartlet shells to a baking sheet and refrigerate for at least 30 minutes before baking (this prevents the tartlet dough from shrinking too much).

3. Preheat the oven to 350°. Bake for 20 to 25 minutes or until the surface of the dough looks dry and no longer shiny. Let the tartlet shells cool completely before removing carefully from the pans. Place approximately 2 tablespoons toasted pecans in the bottom of each cooled tartlet shell.

4. To make the butter caramel filling: In a medium, heavy-bottomed saucepan, combine the sugar and corn syrup over low heat. Cook until the mixture turns a medium-amber color (the corn syrup will help prevent the sugar from crystallizing). Remove from the heat, and then with your hand and arm covered, carefully stir in the cream. The mixture will splatter and bubble up, so stand back! If the caramel has lumps, return the pot to medium-high heat and stir continuously until the lumps are melted. Remove from the heat and stir in the butter until smooth and let sit at room temperature until slightly thickened and cool enough to touch. For best results, the consistency of the caramel should be similar to thick honey. (At this point the caramel can be covered and refrigerated up to 5 days. Carefully warm the caramel before proceeding.) Divide the warm caramel among the tartlet shells, filling each tartlet half full. Set aside.

5. To make the chocolate ganache: In a small saucepan, bring the cream to the scalding point over medium-high heat. In a heat-resistant bowl, combine the bittersweet chocolate, semisweet chocolate, and corn syrup. Pour the scalded cream over the chocolate mixture and gently whisk until the chocolate is completely melted and smooth. Transfer to a small bowl and let cool until slightly thickened, but still pourable. For best results, the consistency of the ganache should be similar to thick honey. (At this point the ganache can be stored, covered and refrigerated, up to 5 days. Carefully warm the ganache before proceeding.) Fill each of the tartlet shells to the rim with the warm chocolate ganache. Immediately place pecans around the outer edge of the tartlets, making a decorative 1/2-inch border of nuts. Refrigerate until firm before serving. The tartlets are best eaten at room temperature, but will keep for several days in the refrigerator.

TARTE AU CHÈVRE AVEC DES POIRES

Goat Cheese Tart with Pears

Fruit and cheese tarts, with a flavor and texture a bit like cheesecake, are popular in France, but there, they are most often made with fromage blanc, *a spreadable cow's milk cheese similar to cream cheese. Making it with goat cheese is our California twist—and our tribute to Laura Chenel, who brought superb goat cheese to California. I think the addition of goat cheese gives the filling a nice tanginess that sets off the fruit. We weren't at all sure whether a goat's-milk cheese dessert tart would go over so well with our customers, but here we are three years later, still baking it every day. You can vary the fresh fruit according to whatever is in season: Huckleberries, figs and raspberries, apricots, peaches, nectarines, and plums all work beautifully. Or you can serve it with fresh fruit on the side and a glass of Sauternes, or with walnuts and a glass of port.*

---

4 ounces (¹/₂ cup) firmly packed goat cheese, at room temperature

6 ounces (³/₄ cup) firmly packed cream cheese, at room temperature

¹/₄ cup plus 4 teaspoons sugar

2 teaspoons heavy whipping cream

¹/₂ teaspoon vanilla extract

¹/₂ teaspoon freshly grated orange zest

1 extra-large egg, separated

1 prebaked shallow 9-inch Pâte Sucrée tart shell (page 114)

1 Anjou pear, quartered, cored, and thinly sliced

¹/₄ cup fresh huckleberries

MAKES ONE 9-INCH TART

1. Preheat the oven to 325°. In the bowl of an electric mixer fitted with the paddle attachment, combine the goat cheese and cream cheese on medium speed until smooth and free of lumps. Add ¹/₄ cup of the sugar and beat on medium speed until combined, scraping down the sides and the bottom of the bowl as needed. Reduce the speed to low and add the heavy cream, vanilla, and orange zest; mix until combined. Increase the speed to medium and continue to mix for 1 minute, scraping down the sides and the bottom of the bowl a couple of times. Add the egg yolk and beat until the yolk is completely incorporated. Set aside.

2. In a clean mixer bowl, using the whisk attachment, whip the egg white on medium speed until foamy. Increase the speed to high and gradually add the remaining 4 teaspoons sugar. Continue to whip to stiff peaks— the whites should be firm and shiny. Using a large flexible spatula, gently fold the whipped egg white into the cheese mixture. Transfer the cheese mixture into the tart shell and, using a flexible spatula, spread the filling over the bottom as evenly as possible. Evenly space the pear slices around the edge of the tart, cut-sides up. Decorate the center of the tart with the huckleberries.

3. Bake in the center of the oven for 25 minutes or until the surface looks dry and the filling is slightly puffed. Cool the tart completely on a wire rack before removing from the pan. Slice into wedges and serve. The tart is best the day it is baked but it can be covered and refrigerated up to 2 days.

GALETTE DES ROIS
Kings' Epiphany Cake

In France, this golden crown of puff pastry with a creamy almond filling is the traditional dessert of Epiphany, or Twelfth Night (January 6), the day the three kings visited the baby Jesus. To add to the fun of the celebration, little charms are traditionally baked into the cake—we use miniature figurines from Santon pottery, in Provence. The lucky person who gets the piece of cake with the charm wins a crown and is king for the day. Our version has a fluffier filling than most, because we lighten the classic frangipane with a bit of pastry cream. This dessert is only as good as the puff pastry it's made with, so I advise you to make it from scratch. When you taste the result, you'll have a little private epiphany of your own.

1. Divide the puff pastry dough in half. Keep one piece refrigerated and roll out the other until ⅛-inch thick. Cut out an 11-inch circle. Repeat rolling and cutting with the remaining dough half. Transfer one of the puff pastry rounds to a parchment paper–lined baking sheet, cover with a piece of parchment paper, and place the second pastry round over the parchment. Keep refrigerated while you make the filling.

2. To make the filling: In the bowl of an electric mixer fitted with the paddle attachment, cream the almonds, sugar, and butter on high speed for 3 minutes, scraping down the sides and the bottom of the bowl as needed. Add the pastry cream, egg, flour, and almond extract and mix on medium speed for 3 minutes, stopping once midway to scrape down the sides and the bottom of the bowl. The filling should be very light and fluffy.

3. To assemble the galette: Take the baking sheet out of the refrigerator, and set aside the top puff pastry round on the parchment. Spread 1½ cups of the filling on the remaining pastry round, leaving a 1-inch border free of filling. Using a pastry brush, brush the border with the egg wash. Hide the charm by tucking it into the filling. Top with the remaining pastry round and press firmly to seal. With a small, sharp knife, score the top with five vertical cuts and five horizontal cuts. Brush the top with egg wash and refrigerate the remaining egg wash for later. Place the galette in the refrigerator for about 1 hour or until the dough is firm. (At this point, the galette can be kept, wrapped airtight and refrigerated, up to 1 day or frozen up to 1 month.)

4. About 20 minutes before baking, preheat the oven to 350°. Just before baking, brush the remaining egg wash on the top of the galette. Bake for 35 to 40 minutes or until the puff pastry has risen and is a deep golden brown. Cool on a wire rack. To serve, cut into wedges with a serrated knife. The galette will keep for a day, but it's best served warm, the day it is made.

1 pound Puff Pastry Dough (page 38)

FILLING

3 ounces (¾ cup) very finely ground almonds

6 tablespoons sugar

2 ounces (4 tablespoons) unsalted butter, at room temperature

¼ cup cold Crème Pâtissière (page 115)

1 extra-large egg, at room temperature

¼ cup plus 1 tablespoon all-purpose flour

½ teaspoon almond extract

1 extra-large egg, well beaten, for egg wash

MAKES ONE 11-INCH CAKE

GÂTEAU BASQUE

Basque Cake

At its best and most traditional, Gâteau Basque is really more cream than cake—a generous layer of dense, creamy custard sandwiched between a simple, homey pastry crust. It comes from southwestern France near Spain, where it's usually eaten with a jam of little cherries from the same area. Our idea at Boulangerie Bay Bread was to put the jam right inside to make individual slices of the cake more portable.

PASTRY

4 ounces (¹/₂ cup) unsalted butter, at room temperature

¹/₂ cup sugar

Freshly grated zest of 1 lemon

¹/₈ teaspoon salt

1 extra-large egg

1 extra-large egg yolk

1¹/₂ cups all-purpose flour

1 teaspoon baking powder

FILLING

¹/₄ cup plus 2 tablespoons sugar

¹/₄ cup all-purpose flour

4 extra-large egg yolks

1³/₄ cups whole milk

¹/₂ vanilla bean, split lengthwise and scraped

1 tablespoon light rum

¹/₂ teaspoon almond extract

³/₄ cup black cherry preserves

1 egg, beaten, for egg wash

MAKES ONE 9-INCH CAKE

1. To make the pastry: In the bowl of an electric mixer fitted with the paddle attachment, cream the butter, sugar, lemon zest, and salt on low speed, until smooth. Add the egg and egg yolk and mix until blended. In a small bowl, whisk together the flour and baking powder. Add the flour mixture to the butter mixture and mix on low speed until a soft dough forms. Turn the dough out onto a lightly floured work surface and divide it into two pieces. Wrap in plastic wrap, and refrigerate until firm, at least 30 minutes.

2. To make the filling: In a medium bowl, whisk together the sugar and flour. Add the egg yolks and ¹/₄ cup of the milk and whisk until smooth. In a medium saucepan, heat the remaining 1¹/₂ cups milk with the vanilla bean and its scrapings, until steaming. While whisking, pour ¹/₂ cup of the hot milk into the yolk mixture. Whisk the yolk mixture back into the hot milk and cook over medium heat, whisking, until boiling and thick, about 4 minutes. Strain the filling through a fine-mesh sieve into a bowl. Discard the vanilla bean. Stir in the rum and almond extract. Place a piece of plastic wrap directly on the surface of the pastry cream to prevent a skin from forming and refrigerate until cool, at least 2 hours and up to 8 hours.

3. Preheat the oven to 325°. Set a 9-inch-diameter flan ring with 1-inch sides on a baking sheet lined with parchment paper. Spray the inside of the pan with vegetable oil spray. Working between two pieces of plastic wrap, roll out the larger disk of dough to an 11-inch round. Remove the plastic wrap and ease the dough into the flan ring, pressing it into the corners and leaving the overhang. Spread the preserves evenly over the bottom of the pastry shell. Add the pastry cream in dollops and then carefully spread it over the preserves. Working between two more pieces of plastic wrap, roll out the second disk of dough to a 10-inch round and lay it over the pastry cream. Press the edges of the top and bottom crust together and cut off the overhang using the back edge of a knife. Using the tines of a fork, lightly score the top crust in a crosshatch pattern. Brush the top of the tart with the remaining egg wash. With the tip of a knife, poke three holes in the top to allow steam to escape.

4. Bake in the center of the oven for 55 minutes, or until the top is golden brown. Transfer the baking sheet to a wire rack and let the tart cool completely. Serve at room temperature or chilled, cut into wedges.

TARTE AU RIZ AVEC DES ABRICOTS

Apricot Rice Tart

I love rice pudding, so I came up with a way to turn it into a tart. At first, we made it with rum-soaked raisins the way my mom used to make her pudding. But eventually we started using fresh apricots for their bright color and tangy flavor, which cuts through the creaminess of the rice. Be careful not to overbake the tart. It should be just set enough to handle, but still very creamy and moist.

1. Preheat the oven to 325°. In a small saucepan, bring the milk, rice, vanilla bean and its scrapings, and salt to a boil over medium heat, stirring occasionally to keep the rice from sticking to the bottom of the pan. Reduce the heat and simmer the mixture, still stirring occasionally, until most of the liquid has been absorbed, about 20 minutes. Remove from the heat and discard the vanilla bean. Stir in the butter. In a medium bowl, whisk together the egg, egg yolk, and sugar. Whisk one-fourth of the hot rice mixture into the egg mixture, and then whisk the tempered mixture into the saucepan with the remaining rice mixture. Cut the apricots in half, remove their pits, and then cut into bite-sized pieces. Scatter the apricot pieces evenly over the bottom of the prebaked tart shell. Pour the rice mixture over the apricots and spread as evenly as possible.

2. Bake in the middle of the oven for 25 minutes or until the center of the tart is set when lightly jiggled. If desired, the baked tart can be placed under the broiler for a few seconds to brown the top slightly. Cool in the pan, on a wire rack. Cut into wedges and serve either warm or chilled.

Variation: Substitute ¾ cup golden raisins macerated in ¼ cup rum for the apricots. A quick way to infuse the rum's flavor into the raisins is to heat them in a microwave oven for 40 seconds on high power. When cool enough to handle, squeeze a little of the excess liquid out and scatter them evenly in the tart shell.

1³/₄ cups milk

¹/₃ cup long-grain white rice

¹/₄ vanilla bean, split lengthwise
  and scraped

Pinch of salt

1¹/₂ ounces (3 tablespoons) unsalted
  butter

1 extra-large egg

1 extra-large egg yolk

¹/₄ cup sugar

3 to 4 fresh, ripe apricots

1 prebaked, shallow 9-inch Pâte
  Sucrée tart shell (page 114)

MAKES ONE 9-INCH TART

GÂTEAU RENVERSÉ AUX ANANAS

Pineapple Upside-Down Cake

Although there is nothing remotely French about this recipe, it's still a favorite at our American Boulangerie. The recipe comes from one of our pastry chefs, who remembers her grandmother making it in a cast-iron skillet. We use a lighter cake pan, but the results are still outstanding: a dense, buttery cake with a rich, caramelized pineapple top. It's fantastic served warm, right out of the pan, with vanilla ice cream.

TOPPING

8 ounces (1 cup) unsalted butter, at room temperature

1 cup firmly packed dark brown sugar

FRUIT

$1/2$ medium pineapple, peeled, cored, halved, and cut into $1/2$-inch-thick slices

CAKE

$1^1/2$ cups plus 1 tablespoon all-purpose flour

2 teaspoons baking powder

$1/2$ teaspoon salt

8 ounces (1 cup) unsalted butter, at room temperature

1 cup firmly packed dark brown sugar

4 extra-large eggs, at room temperature

$1/2$ cup lightly toasted, chopped walnuts (optional)

MAKES ONE 10-INCH CAKE

1. To make the topping: In a small saucepan, melt the butter over low heat. Whisk in the brown sugar and continue cooking, whisking constantly, until the sugar is dissolved and the mixture is combined. Pour into the bottom of a 10-inch cake pan with sides at least $1^1/2$ inches deep. (Do not use a springform pan or the topping will leak out.) Set aside to cool. It is important to let the topping set up, otherwise the fruit and cake batter will sink. (The pan can be prepared up to this point and kept at room temperature for up to 1 day.)

2. To make the fruit layer: Arrange the pineapple slices in a circular design on top of the set topping. Set aside.

3. To make the cake: Preheat the oven to 350°. Sift together the all-purpose flour, baking powder, and salt over a piece of parchment or a medium bowl. Set aside. In the bowl of an electric mixer fitted with the paddle attachment, cream the butter and brown sugar on medium speed until light and fluffy. Scrape down the sides and the bottom of the bowl as necessary. On low speed, add the eggs, one at a time, scraping down the bowl after each addition and beating until combined. Slowly add the flour mixture to the butter and egg mixture and mix on low speed until well combined. Stir in the nuts, and carefully dollop the cake batter over the fruit in the pan, smoothing out the batter with a flexible spatula. Place the pan on a sturdy baking sheet and bake for 40 to 45 minutes or until a toothpick inserted into the center of the cake comes out clean. Cool in the pan, on a wire rack, for 20 to 25 minutes. Invert a serving platter over the cake and, using both hands, firmly grab both the cake pan and the platter and flip them over. Gently lift up the cake pan, scrape off any fruit that might have stuck to the bottom of the pan, and place it back on the cake. Let cool slightly. Serve warm, with whipped cream if desired. If not serving within 2 to 3 hours after baking, leave the cake in the pan and reheat briefly over a low burner on the stove to soften topping, before inverting cake and removing pan.

GÂTEAU DE MAÏS RENVERSÉ AUX PÊCHES

Peach Cornmeal Upside-Down Cake

Here is another satisfying Gâteau à l'Americain. *The cornmeal in the batter helps soak up some of the juice from the peaches and adds a bit of crunch to contrast with the soft, caramelized fruit. Make this in the summertime, when fresh peaches are at their best—or try substituting other summer fruits, like nectarines or pitted bing cherries. Be sure not to overbake this cake, so it stays moist and soft.*

1. To make the topping: In a small saucepan, melt the butter over low heat. Whisk in the brown sugar and continue cooking, whisking constantly, until the sugar is dissolved and the mixture is combined. Pour into the bottom of a 10-inch cake pan with sides at least 1½ inches deep. (Do not use a springform pan or the topping will leak out.) Set aside to cool. It is important to let the topping set up, otherwise the fruit and cake batter will sink. (The pan can be prepared up to this point and kept at room temperature for up to 1 day.)

2. To make the fruit layer: Peel the peaches. Cut in half, remove the pits, and then cut each half into ½-inch-thick wedges. Arrange the peach wedges in a circular design on top of the set topping. Set aside.

3. To make the cake: Preheat the oven to 350°. In a small bowl, stir together flour, cornmeal, baking powder, and salt. Set aside. In the bowl of an electric mixer fitted with the paddle attachment, cream the butter and sugar on medium speed until light and fluffy. Scrape down the sides and bottom of the bowl as needed. Reduce the speed to low and add the eggs and the yolk, one at a time, stopping to scrape the bowl after each addition. With the mixer on low speed, slowly add the flour mixture to the butter and egg mixture and mix, stopping once to scrape down the bowl, until well combined. Carefully dollop the cake batter over the fruit in the pan, smoothing the batter with a flexible spatula. Place on a sturdy baking sheet and bake for 50 to 55 minutes or until a toothpick inserted into the center of the cake comes out clean. Cool the cake for 20 minutes to 25 minutes on a wire rack. Invert a serving platter over the cake and, using both hands, firmly grab both the cake pan and the platter and flip them over. Gently lift up the cake pan, scrape off any fruit that might have stuck to the bottom of the pan, and place it back on the cake. Let cool slightly. Serve warm, with whipped cream if desired. If not serving within 2 to 3 hours after baking, leave the cake in the pan and reheat briefly over a low burner on the stove to soften topping, before inverting the cake and removing the pan.

TOPPING

8 ounces (1 cup) unsalted butter, at room temperature

1 cup firmly packed light brown sugar

FRUIT

2 extra-large, ripe peaches

CAKE

1 cup all-purpose flour

²/₃ cup yellow cornmeal

1½ teaspoons baking powder

¼ teaspoon salt

8 ounces (1 cup) unsalted butter, at room temperature

1 cup granulated sugar

4 extra-large eggs, at room temperature

1 extra-large egg yolk

MAKES ONE 10-INCH CAKE

GÂTEAU FONDANT AU CHOCOLAT
Bittersweet Chocolate Cake

This is the only chocolate cake we make, and once you try it, it might become the only one you make, too. Its stroke of genius is marbling ganache into the already ultra-chocolatey cake batter. It may not be the most spectacular-looking cake when it comes out of the oven, but once you slice it and present it on a nice plate with a big dollop of whipped cream, it's something truly beautiful. I highly recommend warming each slice for a few seconds in the microwave just before garnishing and serving: The ganache will soften and the flavors will become even more intense.

1. Preheat the oven to 325°. Spray a 10-inch springform pan with vegetable oil spray and line the bottom with a circle of parchment paper. Set aside.

2. In a large, heat-resistant bowl set over a pot of simmering water, melt the chocolate and butter, stirring occasionally. Remove the bowl from the heat and whisk in the cocoa powder. In a small bowl, whisk the egg yolks to break them up, and then whisk into the chocolate mixture. Set aside.

3. In the bowl of an electric mixer fitted with the whisk attachment, whip the egg whites and salt on medium speed until foamy. Increase the speed to high and gradually add the sugar. Continue to whip to medium-firm peaks—the peaks will droop slightly when you lift up the whisk. Stir the egg whites, rather vigorously, into the warm chocolate mixture, until there are no white streaks visible. You need not be gentle, as this cake is best without a lot of air incorporated into it. Transfer the batter to the prepared pan, smooth it out, and pour the ganache on top. Using a spoon, or your fingers, marble the ganache into the batter.

4. Bake in the center of the oven for 35 to 40 minutes or until the center of the cake no longer looks shiny. The cake will be puffed up and wobbly in the center but set on the edges. It's a soft cake that will firm up as it cools. Cool the cake completely, on a wire rack, before removing the side from the pan.

5. To slice the cake (easiest when it is chilled), run a long knife under hot water, then wipe it off with a towel, and cut the cake into 12 slices. The cake can be kept 3 days at room temperature or up to 5 days if refrigerated.

12 ounces bittersweet chocolate, finely chopped (approximately 2 cups)

4 ounces ($^1/_2$ cup) unsalted butter

2 tablespoons unsweetened cocoa powder

4 extra-large eggs, separated

2 extra-large egg whites

Pinch of salt

$^1/_2$ cup sugar

$^1/_2$ cup chocolate ganache (page 104), melted

MAKES ONE 10-INCH CAKE

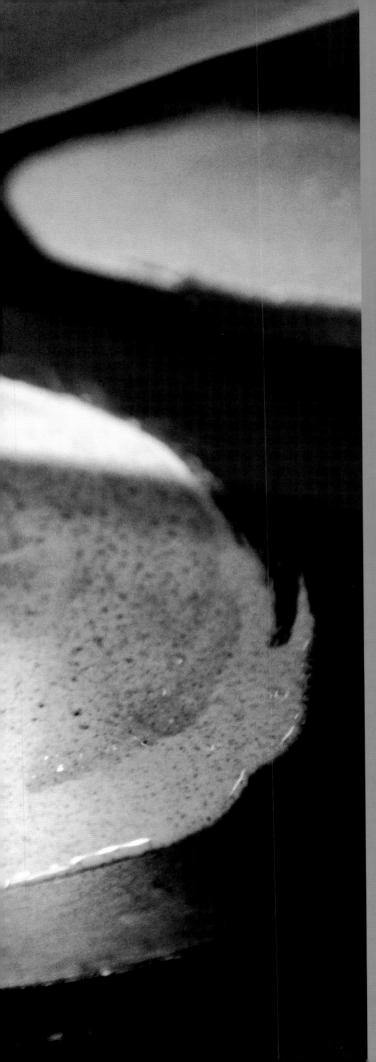

GALETTES ET CRÊPES
Pancakes

Crêpes have a strange and wonderful effect on me. They make me feel like I'm on vacation. Maybe it's because my first and happiest crêpe memories are from trips to the beach as a little kid. After a long day of running around in the sun and playing in the water, nothing could possibly have tasted better than a warm crêpe, wrapped in a piece of waxed paper, with lots of salted butter and sugar in the middle.

Eventually I went to Brittany, where they take their crêpes very seriously. For me, the cuisine, the culture, and the landscape there have always felt like another country altogether. It was in Brittany where I learned to appreciate more sophisticated, perfectly cooked, crispy-edged crêpes with all kinds of wonderful fillings—and especially the buckwheat galettes for which the region is famous. I still think it's a big treat to eat them when I'm there.

In France, generally speaking, crêpes have sweet fillings and can be found throughout the country, while galettes have savory fillings and are pretty much confined to Brittany. You might find exceptions to this in Paris, but then, you can find exceptions to everything in Paris.

A few years ago, we decided to open a little *crêperie* in San Francisco, around the corner from our Boulangerie Bay Bread. We called it Galette, and with its design, colors, and even the little take-away window on the street, we hoped to give people a bit of that happy, summer-vacation feeling that, for us, seems so perfectly connected with crêpes.

*We dedicate this chapter to
the memory of our dear colleague Fabrice.*

GALETTES
Buckwheat Crêpes

This recipe makes the kind of lacy-edged crêpes that are served with savory fillings in Brittany. The buckwheat adds a nutty flavor and a rustic, toasty brown look that goes perfectly with a wide range of ingredients, such as thinly sliced or chopped cooked meats, seafood, sautéed vegetables, and cheeses.

1¼ cups buckwheat flour, sifted

1 cup plus 2 tablespoons all-purpose flour, sifted

1½ teaspoons salt

3 extra-large eggs

2 cups plus 1 tablespoon water

1¼ cups whole milk

¾ ounce (1½ tablespoons) unsalted butter, melted

Vegetable oil, as needed for pan

MAKES SIXTEEN CRÊPES

1. In a medium bowl, whisk together the buckwheat flour, all-purpose flour, and salt. Create a little well in the middle of the flour mixture, and crack the eggs into it. Using a whisk, mix the eggs in a circular motion, incorporating the flour mixture very slowly. When the batter is too stiff to whisk easily, slowly add the water and milk to the center of the wet batter, trying to keep the mixture lump free. Press the batter through a fine-mesh strainer and let rest at room temperature for 1 hour before using. Alternatively, cover and refrigerate the batter up to 2 days. When ready to cook the batter, return it to room temperature, if chilled, and whisk in the melted butter.

2. Using a paper towel, apply a light layer of oil over the bottom of a 10-inch nonstick pan. Heat the pan over medium-high heat. When it is hot, stir the batter and, using a ¼-cup measure, ladle the batter into the pan. The batter should "sing" a little bit and begin to set if the pan is ready. Lift the pan by its handle and quickly tilt and swirl it so that the batter coats the entire bottom of the pan. Do this quickly or the batter will set before the bottom of the pan is coated. Return the pan to the heat and cook about 1 minute, until lacy golden brown, then loosen the edges with a heat-resistant spatula and flip the crêpe. Cook about 20 seconds longer, or until the bottom has browned. Turn the crêpe out onto a plate and return the pan to the heat. Continue making crêpes, stirring the batter before each one to make sure the flour is evenly distributed and reapplying oil to the pan as needed to prevent sticking. As you make the crêpes, stack them one on top of the other, with the side browned first face-down, so when they are filled and folded the prettier side will be visible. If not using immediately, wrap the entire stack in plastic wrap and refrigerate up to 2 days or layer between sheets of parchment paper and freeze up to 1 month. Bring to room temperature before using.

GALETTES AVEC JAMBON ET FROMAGE
Buckwheat Crêpes with Ham and Cheese

This is probably the most popular of all the savory crêpes in France. Use a good-quality ham, sliced paper thin, and the best Gruyère you can find. I also like prosciutto with Brie or Bayonne ham with Etorki, a Basque sheeps' milk cheese from the French Pyrénées mountains. I like to serve this with a good-quality mustard on the side and a crisp green salad.

Olive oil, as needed for pan

4 cooked Galettes (page 144)

10 ounces grated Swiss Gruyère
 cheese (about 1¹/₄ cups)

8 ounces thinly sliced ham (about
 8 slices)

MAKES FOUR FILLED CRÊPES

1. Using a paper towel, apply a light layer of olive oil over the bottom of a 10-inch nonstick pan. Place a cooked buckwheat crêpe in the pan, prettiest-side down. Spread one-fourth of the grated cheese evenly over the entire surface of the crêpe and top with one-fourth of the ham (about 2 slices). Gently heat the crêpe over medium heat; you want to heat it just long enough to melt the cheese but not overcook the crêpe. While still in the pan, fold the crêpe into a square: Bring together the right and left edges to meet in the middle, then bring together the top and bottom edges to meet in the middle. Flip the folded crêpe over and continue cooking the opposite side until heated through, about 2 minutes.

2. Carefully slide the crêpe onto a serving plate. Repeat cooking with the remaining crêpes and fillings, reapplying oil to the pan for each crêpe. Serve immediately.

GALETTES AUX POULET, EPINARDS, ET À LA MOUTARDE EN GRAINS

Buckwheat Crêpes with Chicken, Spinach, and Whole-Grain Mustard

This substantial crêpe—really a whole meal in itself—is our best-seller at Galette. The mustard is critical. Find yourself a really good one, and don't be shy about using plenty of it. I even like to serve this with a little extra mustard on the side. Accompany with a salad of crisp fresh greens.

1. Season the chicken breasts with salt and pepper. In a large sauté pan, heat 2 tablespoons olive oil over medium-high heat. Add the chicken and sauté until golden brown, 3 to 4 minutes per side. Remove from pan and set aside. Add the spinach to the pan and cook just until wilted, 2 to 3 minutes. Remove from pan and set aside. Add the cream and cook over medium-high heat, scraping to dissolve any chicken drippings on the bottom of the pan, until the cream is slightly reduced, about 3 minutes. Reduce heat to low, whisk in the mustard, and set aside. Cut the chicken into bite-sized pieces, then return the chicken and spinach to the cream in the pan and simmer over low heat until the chicken is cooked through, 3 to 5 minutes. Season to taste with salt and pepper. Keep warm.

2. Using a paper towel, apply a light layer of olive oil over the bottom of a 10-inch nonstick pan. Place a cooked buckwheat crêpe in the pan, prettiest-side down. Place about ¾ cup of the chicken filling in the middle of the crêpe and spread it out just a bit with the back of a spoon. Gently heat the crêpe over medium heat about 1 minute, until heated through. While still in the pan, fold the crêpe into a square: Bring together the right and left edges to meet in the middle, then bring together the top and bottom edges to meet in the middle. Carefully slide the crêpe onto a plate and dollop with a bit of the remaining filling; this is a good way to hide any imperfections! Repeat with the remaining crêpes and filling.

3. Serve immediately.

4 small boneless chicken breasts (about 1 pound)

Salt and freshly ground black pepper

2 tablespoons olive oil, plus additional for pan

2 bunches spinach, washed and tough stems removed

1½ cups heavy cream

2 tablespoons whole-grain mustard, or more to taste

4 cooked Galettes (page 144)

MAKES FOUR FILLED CRÊPES

GALETTES aux FRUITS de MER

Buckwheat Crêpes with Seafood

As with many simple recipes, a few little tricks will make this perfect. The first of these is the method for searing and deglazing. While you don't want to fully cook the seafood in the hot pan initially, you do want it to take on some color and to leave some browned bits in the pan. To accomplish this, use high heat and cook in small batches, because overcrowding will cause the seafood to steam, not sear. Second, use a thick, gooey, high-quality cream. Look for one that comes from a local dairy and is pasteurized rather than ultra-pasteurized. Finally, you can use all kinds of fresh seafood—including lobster, crab, prawns, and oysters—but whatever you choose, it's important to avoid overcooking. After searing, remove the seafood and, using the same sauté pan, bring the cream to a rolling boil and reduce it. Return the partially cooked seafood, stirring gently for no longer than two minutes. The seafood will finish cooking in the cream.

---

1 tablespoon unsalted butter

1 pound fresh mushrooms, thinly sliced

2 tablespoons olive oil, plus additional for pan

8 large sea scallops, or 1 pound bay scallops

4 tiger prawns, peeled and halved lengthwise

2 tablespoons Calvados, apple brandy, brandy, or whiskey

1 cup heavy cream

1 pound steamed mussels, shells removed

Salt and freshly ground black pepper

4 cooked Galettes (page 144)

MAKES FOUR FILLED CRÊPES

1. In a medium sauté pan, melt the butter over high heat. Add the mushrooms and sauté until lightly browned and all their liquid has evaporated, about 5 minutes. Transfer to a small bowl and set aside. In the same pan, heat oil over high heat. Add the scallops and prawns and sauté just until golden on both sides. Using tongs or a slotted spoon, transfer the scallops and prawns to a plate as they finish browning.

2. Remove pan from the heat and add the Calvados (see the sidebar on page 155 for flambé safety tips). Heat the Calvados over high heat until hot, about 30 seconds. Remove the pan from the heat, and carefully, at arm's length, tilt the pan to light the Calvados with the gas flame or a match. Stand back—be careful of the flame! Once the flames have died down, return the pan to high heat, add the cream, and bring to a boil. Continue to cook, scraping the bottom of the pan to dissolve any of the browned seafood drippings, until the sauce has reduced by half. Add the mussels, scallops, prawns, and mushrooms, with their collected juices, to the pan and simmer, stirring gently, about 2 minutes, or until the mixture is heated through. Season to taste with salt and pepper. Keep warm.

3. Using a paper towel, apply a light layer of olive oil over the bottom of a 10-inch nonstick pan. Place a cooked buckwheat crêpe in the pan, prettiest-side down. Place about ¾ cup of the seafood filling in the middle of the crêpe and spread it out with the back of a spoon. Gently heat the crêpe over medium heat about 1 minute, until heated through. Fold the crêpe into a square: Bring together the right and left edges to meet in the middle, then bring together the top and bottom edges to meet in the middle. Carefully slide the crêpe onto a plate and dollop with a bit of the remaining filling; this is a good way to hide any imperfections! Repeat with the remaining crêpes and filling, reapplying oil as needed to the pan. Serve immediately.

CRÊPES AU BEURRE SALÉ ET AU SUCRE

When you're ordering one of these in France, you just say, "Beurre-sucre, s'il vous plait." This is definitely my favorite crêpe—simple, soft, sweet, warm, and beautiful. It's the crêpe I first fell in love with, and I recommend it for introducing your kids to crêpes, too. You can make the crêpes a day ahead of time. Just warm them one at a time, prettiest side down, in a 10-inch, nonstick sauté pan over medium heat about 1 minute. Spear 1 tablespoon of butter with a fork and rub it all over each crêpe until there are no dry spots, and the butter is completely melted. Sprinkle one-half of the crêpe with 1 teaspoon of the sugar. When the crêpe is heated through and the sugar is still a bit crunchy, about 1 minute, fold the crêpe in half and then fold in half again and eat immediately, or for a crowd, carefully slide them onto a serving plate, brush them with a little butter, and warm them in the broiler. If you want to try a great variation, spread them with honey and lemon juice (and, of course, plenty of salted butter, too).

CRÊPE PANS

Having the right sort of pan is a great advantage when making crêpes. If you make them often, consider buying a crêpe pan and dedicating it solely to this purpose. A typical crêpe pan is a flat heavy skillet with shallow, sloping sides and a long, narrow handle that makes it easy to lift the pan and swirl the batter. Newer crêpe pans are available in nonstick finishes, which makes turning the crêpes (I use a heat-proof flexible spatula for this) a breeze. You can also use any good-quality 10-inch skillet, but make sure it has a nonstick finish and gently sloping sides. A straight-sided pan would make it difficult to ease the spatula under the finished side when flipping.

CRÊPES

Crêpes

This is the basic batter for our sweet crêpes at Galette. It's very versatile and can be used for anything from simple butter-and-sugar crêpes to blintzes or flambéed dessert crêpes. Let the batter rest for at least an hour and have it at room temperature when you're ready to use it, you may have to thin it a bit after it has rested. If it seems too thick, add water, a teaspoon or two at a time, until you get a fluid, pourable batter, about the consistency of buttermilk. For greasing the pan with oil, butter, or a combination of both, you can apply a light layer using a piece of paper towel, but I like to use a small potato, cut in half and speared onto the end of a fork. I never use a pastry brush, which can shed its bristles into the food and singe. Crêpes can be made ahead of time, stacked, wrapped tightly, and refrigerated or frozen. If you want to use just a few at a time, you can freeze them with sheets of parchment or waxed paper between each crêpe.

---

1. Sift the flour into a medium bowl, then whisk in the sugar and salt. Create a little well in the middle of the flour mixture, and crack the eggs into it. Using a whisk, mix the eggs in a circular motion, incorporating the flour mixture very slowly. When the batter is too stiff to whisk easily, slowly add the milk to the center of the wet batter, trying to keep the mixture lump free. Once all the milk has been incorporated, whisk in the vanilla and rum. Press the batter through a fine-mesh strainer and let rest at room temperature for 1 hour before using. Alternatively, cover and refrigerate the batter up to 2 days. When ready to cook the batter, return it to room temperature, if chilled, and whisk in the melted butter.

2. Using a paper towel, apply a light layer of the oil over the bottom of a 10-inch nonstick pan. Heat the pan over medium-high heat. When it is hot, stir the batter and, using a ¼-cup measure, ladle batter into the pan. The batter should "sing" a little bit and begin to set if the pan is ready. Lift the pan by its handle, and quickly tilt and swirl it so the batter coats the entire bottom of the pan; do this quickly or the batter will set before the bottom of the pan is coated. Return the pan to the heat and cook about 1 minute, until lacy golden brown, then loosen the edges with a heat-resistant spatula and flip the crêpe. Cook about 20 seconds longer, or until the bottom has browned. Turn the crêpe out onto a plate and return the pan to the heat. Continue making crêpes, stirring the batter before each one to make sure the flour is evenly distributed and reapplying oil to the pan as needed to prevent sticking. As you finish cooking the crêpes, stack them one on top of the other, with the side browned first face-down, so when they are filled and folded this prettier side will be visible. If not using immediately, wrap the entire stack in plastic wrap and refrigerate up to 2 days or layer between sheets of parchment paper and freeze up to 1 month. Bring to room temperature before using.

3¾ cups all-purpose flour

½ cup plus 3 tablespoons sugar

2 teaspoons salt

4 extra-large eggs

5⅓ cups milk

2 teaspoons vanilla extract

1 tablespoon rum

1½ ounces (3 tablespoons) unsalted butter, melted

Vegetable oil, as needed for pan

MAKES EIGHTEEN CRÊPES

CRÊPES AVEC POMMES CARAMELISÈES ET FLAMBÉES AU CALVADOS

Crêpes with Caramelized Apple and Calvados Flambé

This is a traditional favorite in the style of Benodet, a town in southern Brittany. It's also very good made with fresh apricots in place of the apples. Serve with vanilla ice cream and a glass of ice-cold French cider.

4 Granny Smith or other firm apples (about 2 pounds), peeled and cored

2 ounces (4 tablespoons) unsalted butter

4 tablespoons sugar

2 to 4 tablespoons Calvados, apple brandy, or Cognac

Vegetable oil, as needed for pan

4 cooked Crêpes (page 151)

Vanilla or caramel ice cream, for serving

MAKES FOUR FILLED CRÊPES

1. Slice the apples into ½-inch-thick slices. In a 10-inch, nonstick sauté pan, melt the butter and the sugar over medium heat. Cook, stirring, until the mixture starts to caramelize. Add the apple slices and cook, stirring occasionally, until they begin to caramelize, about 3 minutes. Remove the pan from the heat, and carefully, at arm's length, tilt the pan to light the Calvados with the gas flame or a match. Stand back—be careful of the flame! Once the flames have died down, return the pan to the heat, and keep the apple mixture warm over low heat. (see page 155 for flambé safety tips).

2. Using a paper towel, apply a light layer of oil over the bottom of a 10-inch nonstick pan. Place a cooked crêpe in the pan, prettiest-side down. Place about ¾ cup of the apple filling in the middle of the crêpe and spread it out just a bit with the back of a spoon. Gently heat the crêpe over medium heat until warm, about 1 minute. While still in the pan, fold the crêpe into an envelope: Bring together the right and left edges to meet in the middle, then bring the bottom edge up to the middle of the crêpe. It will resemble an open envelope with the apples coming out of the top. Carefully slide the crêpe onto a plate and dollop with some of the remaining filling; this is a good way to hide any imperfections! Repeat with the remaining crêpes and filling, reapplying oil as needed to the pan.

3. Accompany with a scoop of vanilla or caramel ice cream, if you wish, and serve immediately.

CRÊPES SUZETTES

Crêpes with Orange Sauce

This is our version of the dramatic Parisian classic, which, some people say, was created over a century ago for actors to eat onstage as part of a play at the Comédie Française. The theatrical element comes, of course, from flaming the alcohol. For best results, use a small pan to bring the liqueur or rum to a boil. Pour the premeasured liquid into the pan off the stovetop to avoid accidents. And remember, drama is fun, but the less you flambé, the better the flavor will be.

3 cups freshly squeezed orange juice

$1/2$ cup sugar

4 prepared Crêpes (page 151)

4 ounces (8 tablespoons) unsalted butter

1 ounce (2 tablespoons) chopped Candied Orange Rind (page 155)

$1/2$ cup Grand Marnier or rum

MAKES FOUR FILLED CRÊPES

1. In a small saucepan, bring the orange juice and sugar to a boil over high heat and cook until reduced to $1^1/2$ cups, 10 to 15 minutes. Keep warm.

2. Warm a cooked crêpe, prettiest-side down, in a 10-inch, nonstick sauté pan over medium heat. Spear 1 tablespoon of the butter with a fork and rub it all over the crêpe until there are no dry spots and the butter is completely melted. When the crêpe is heated through, fold the crêpe in half and then into half again to form a triangle. Carefully slide the crêpe onto a serving plate. Repeat with the remaining crêpes, using 1 tablespoon of the butter for each.

3. Add the remaining 4 tablespoons butter and the candied orange rind to the reduced orange juice and continue to cook, swirling the mixture by moving the pan in a circular motion, until the butter is melted. Remove the pan from the heat, and add the Grand Marnier (see page 155 for flambé safety tips). Carefully, at arm's length, tilt the pan to light the Grand Marnier with the gas flame or a match. Pour immediately, flames and all, over the crêpes and serve at once.

CANDIED ORANGE RIND

1. Using a vegetable peeler, remove the rind from the oranges, taking care to remove as little of the white pith as possible. In a small saucepan, combine the orange rind and 3 cups of the water, and bring to a boil over high heat. As soon as the water boils, remove the orange rinds using a fine-mesh strainer and immerse into a bowl of ice water to stop the cooking. Remove orange rind and repeat this blanching process two more times using 3 cups boiling water each time. Drain.

2. In the same saucepan, combine the remaining 1 cup water, 1 cup of the sugar, and the blanched orange rinds. Bring to a boil over high heat. Reduce the heat and simmer until the rind is translucent and the liquid is slightly thickened, about 10 minutes. Remove the pan from the heat and allow the rinds to cool in the sugar syrup.

3. Using a slotted spoon or strainer, remove the rinds from the sugar syrup and drain for a moment before transferring to a parchment-lined baking sheet or shallow pan. Let the rinds dry slightly, about 1 hour.

4. Sprinkle the remaining $^1/_2$ cup sugar over the dried rinds, and, using your fingers, gently toss to coat them well. Carefully remove the rinds from the sugar, gently shaking them in a fine-mesh strainer to remove any excess. Transfer to a wire rack and let dry completely. The candied orange rinds can be kept in an airtight container, refrigerated or in a cool place, up to 3 months.

CANDIED ORANGE RIND

2 oranges

10 cups water

1$^1/_2$ cups sugar

MAKES ABOUT ONE CUP

FLAMBÉ SAFETY TIPS

Please use caution and common sense when flambéing, the process of pouring warmed liquor over food and lighting it. Make sure children, adults, clothing, and hair are well away from flame's reach. Don't pour straight from the bottle into the pan. Instead, measure out the amount of liquor needed for a recipe into a separate container. Do not add the alcoholic liquid while in close proximity to a gas flame. You want to control the burning process and minimize the possibility of unwanted fire by adding the liquor to the pan away from stove. Then return the pan to the stovetop and, standing as far back as possible, gently tilt it away from you, but toward the flame, to ignite it. The flames will die down as the alcohol burns off.

CRÊPES BELLE-HÉLÈNE
Crêpes Belle-Hélène

Like Crêpes Suzette (page 154), Poire Belle-Hélène, is another grande dame from the world of nineteenth-century French desserts. In French cooking, the name always means poached pears and chocolate sauce—often served with vanilla ice cream or crème anglaise. I love how this combination works with a warm, tender crêpe. For a shortcut, you can use canned pears in light syrup, but don't skimp on the chocolate sauce—make it from scratch with good-quality chocolate.

1. Place the dark chocolate and milk chocolate in a medium, heat-resistant bowl. In a small saucepan, combine the milk and cream and bring to a boil over high heat. Pour the hot milk mixture over the chopped chocolate and whisk until the chocolate is completely melted and smooth. Set aside.

2. Warm a cooked crêpe, prettiest-side down, in a 10-inch, nonstick sauté pan over medium heat. When the crêpe is heated through, place about one-fourth of the pear slices in the middle of the crêpe. Gently heat the crêpe over medium heat until warm, about 1 minute. While still in the pan, fold the crêpe into an envelope: bring together the right and left edges to meet in the middle, then bring the bottom edge up to the middle of the crêpe. It will resemble an open envelope with the pears coming out of the top. Carefully slide the crêpe onto a plate. Repeat with the remaining crêpes and pears.

3. To serve: Drizzle each crêpe generously with chocolate sauce and sprinkle each with ¼ cup almond slices. Add a scoop of ice cream, if you wish, and serve immediately.

6 ounces dark chocolate, finely chopped (about 1 cup)

6 ounces milk chocolate, finely chopped (about 1 cup)

1 cup milk

1 cup heavy cream

4 cooked Crêpes (page 151)

4 Asian, Comice, or Bartlett pears, peeled, halved, cored, and poached; or 1 can (15½ ounces) sliced pears in syrup, drained

1 cup sliced, toasted almonds

Ice cream, preferably caramel, for serving (optional)

MAKES FOUR FILLED CRÊPES

LA PÂTISSERIE DES ENFANTS
Children's Pastries

As a little kid, I was fixated on baking—the smells of the bakery near our house, the springiness of bread dough, and especially the magic of watching simple ingredients being transformed into something completely different and totally delicious. Now that we have three kids I'm experiencing that fascination all over again through their eyes. Baking with children is a great way to get them involved in the kitchen. It gives them a sense of pride and confidence to have everyone in the family go crazy for something they made with their own hands. In this chapter, I have assembled a few of our favorite family recipes that are fun and easy to make together. They're not silly "children's recipes"—just simple recipes that we love. I hope you and the children in your life feel the same way.

CHARLOTTE AUX FRAISES
Individual Strawberry Brioche Charlottes

This is one of the easiest and most satisfying of all summertime desserts, when the weather is hot and the fruit is ripe and sweet. It's made from just three ingredients—bread, berries, and sugar—though you may want to serve it with a little something extra, like a dollop of whipped cream or a spoonful of lemon curd. My kids love to eat this, and they really get into helping line the ramekins with the brioche. Bear in mind that the charlottes must be assembled at least twelve hours in advance of serving time.

1. Halve 1 pint of strawberries. In a small saucepan, combine the halved strawberries and ⅔ cup of the sugar. Bring to a boil over high heat, stirring frequently. Reduce the heat to medium, and cook the berries until they're very soft and falling apart, about 6 minutes. Remove the pan from the heat, and then purée the berries in a blender until smooth. Set aside.

2. Slice the remaining strawberries into ⅛-inch-thick slices. Line the bottom and sides of each ramekin with the slices. Coarsely dice the left-over strawberry slices (you should have about ¼ cup diced strawberries) and reserve. Using a round cookie cutter the same diameter as the ramekins, cut out 12 pieces of brioche. Reserve the scraps for later. Dip 6 of the cut brioche rounds into the strawberry purée, soaking them completely, then place 1 in the bottom of each strawberry-lined ramekin. Line the sides of the ramekins with the reserved brioche scraps, once again soaking them in the strawberry purée first. Trim the bread slices to fit snugly, as needed. Place about 1 tablespoon of the reserved diced strawberries in the center of each ramekin. Soak the remaining brioche rounds in the strawberry purée and then top each ramekin with 1 of the rounds. Gently press down on each completed ramekin. Cover with plastic wrap, and refrigerate overnight.

3. To serve, remove the charlottes by running a knife around the perimeter of the ramekins and inverting each onto a serving plate. Garnish with fresh strawberries.

1½ pints strawberries, hulled

⅔ cup sugar

½ loaf day-old brioche, crusts cut off, sliced ⅜- to ½- inch thick

MAKES SIX 4-OUNCE RAMEKINS

CRÈME CARAMEL
Vanilla Custard with Caramel Sauce

Hallelujah! This is my mother's crème caramel—so no changes allowed! She doesn't use a bain-marie (water bath), so sometimes little holes form all along the sides—a result some purists might consider a flaw. But that's what makes it my mom's, and that's just the way the little kid in me still likes it.

CUSTARD

4 cups milk

1/2 vanilla bean, split and scraped

7 extra-large eggs

2/3 cup sugar

1/4 teaspoon salt

CARAMEL

1/4 cup sugar

MAKES ONE 6-CUP BAKING DISH

1. To make the custard: In a small saucepan, bring the milk and the vanilla bean, with its scrapings, to a simmer over high heat. Remove from the heat and let cool completely. In a medium bowl, whisk together the eggs, sugar, and salt. Whisk in the cooled milk mixture until thoroughly combined. Strain the custard through a fine-mesh sieve into a medium bowl. Cover with plastic wrap and refrigerate for at least 2 hours or overnight.

2. To make the caramel: In a heavy-bottomed saucepan, heat the sugar over medium-high heat. As soon as the sugar starts to melt from underneath, stir it with a long-handled metal spoon so the sugar melts evenly and doesn't burn. The sugar will clump at first, but crush any clumps with your spoon and they will dissolve. Cook the sugar until it becomes medium to dark amber in color. The whole process will take about 5 minutes. Immediately pour the caramel into a 6-cup baking dish (7½ inches in diameter with 3½-inch sides), tilting to make sure the bottom is evenly coated.

3. Preheat the oven to 450°—yes, 450°! Pour the custard into the caramel-coated baking dish. Bake for approximately 40 to 45 minutes or until the custard is slightly firm yet still jiggly in the center, with a light brown skin on the surface. Let cool completely at room temperature before covering and refrigerating overnight.

4. To serve, spoon straight from the dish, not forgetting to scoop out some of the caramel underneath.

PAIN TROUVÉ au FOUR

Baked French Toast

If you like French toast, try it our way—baked not fried. It's called Pain Perdu, *or "lost bread," because it's usually made from stale ends of bread that would otherwise be thrown away. But I call our version* Pain Trouvé *because we make it from slices of day-old brioche. You can also use a good challah, a high-quality white bread, or even a country bread, as they often do in France. The key is to slice it thin, really let it soak, and be liberal in sprinkling the sugar on top so it gets a good crunchy crust. If you want to make this in advance, don't soak it overnight. Instead, bake it completely the night before and then reheat it in the microwave, heating each ramekin for 30 to 40 seconds. Whether you serve it with maple syrup, honey, or fruit preserves, it's always the big hit of the breakfast table.*

1. Preheat the oven to 350°. Lightly spray 6, 4-ounce ramekins with vegetable oil spray. Using a round cookie cutter the same diameter as your ramekins, cut out 18 rounds of brioche. Place 3 rounds of brioche into each ramekin. In a medium bowl, whisk together ½ cup of the sugar and the eggs. Whisk in the milk, cream, and vanilla extract until well combined. Pour ½ cup of this mixture into each ramekin, making sure the brioche is completely soaked. Sprinkle 1 teaspoon of sugar over each ramekin.

2. Arrange the ramekins on a sturdy baking sheet. Bake in the center of the oven for 30 to 35 minutes or until no liquid rises to the surface when the brioche is gently pressed in the center. Let cool in the ramekins, then remove from the ramekins by running a knife around their perimeters and turning the French toasts out of pan. Serve browned-side up, with hot maple syrup or jam.

1 loaf day-old brioche, sliced
 ³/₈ to ¹/₂ inch thick (page 50)

¹/₂ cup plus 2 tablespoons sugar

3 extra-large eggs

1 cup whole milk

1 cup heavy cream

¹/₄ teaspoon vanilla extract

MAKES SIX 4-OUNCE RAMEKINS

TRUFFES au CHOCOLAT

Chocolate Truffles

Kids love to make these, and when you give them a try, you will know why. It's just like making little mud pies. You can make them very simple and classic by rolling them in cocoa powder, or go for a more sophisticated and grown-up approach by adding some lemon or orange zest or liqueur, such as Grand Marnier, to the still-warm ganache and then rolling the shaped truffles in nuts or cocoa powder.

1 cup plus 1 tablespoon heavy cream

4 ounces coarsely chopped semisweet chocolate (about ³/₄ cup)

4 ounces coarsely chopped bittersweet chocolate (about ³/₄ cup)

¹/₂ cup sifted unsweetened cocoa powder or ¹/₂ cup finely chopped toasted nuts, for coating

MAKES TWENTY-FOUR TRUFFLES

1. In a small saucepan, bring the cream to the scalding point over medium heat. Meanwhile, place the semisweet and bittersweet chocolates in a heat-resistant bowl. Pour the scalded cream over the chocolate mixture and gently whisk until the chocolate is completely melted and smooth. Pour the ganache into a shallow pan or container and refrigerate until cold and set, at least 2 hours. Meanwhile, place the cocoa powder or nuts into a shallow dish, line a baking sheet with plastic wrap or parchment paper, and have at hand a dish or container in which to place the finished truffles.

2. If you are right-handed, working from left to right, place the chilled ganache, the lined baking sheet, the dishes of coatings, and the final storage container in a line. Using a small scoop (¹/₂ to 1 inch in diameter) or a spoon, scoop out rough balls of the firm ganache. As they are scooped, place them on the lined baking sheet. (Return the baking sheet to the refrigerator if the balls are getting too soft.) Quickly roll the rough balls of ganache between your hands to form truffles—they don't need to be perfectly smooth and round. Immediately roll them in the desired coating. If necessary, gently shake them in a dry strainer to remove any excess coating. Store, well wrapped, in the refrigerator for up to 10 days.

3. To serve, remove from refrigerator, arrange on a serving plate, and let stand at room temperature for about 30 minutes before serving.

POT de CRÈME au CHOCOLAT
Chocolate Pot de Crème

Is there a kid—or an adult—who doesn't like chocolate pudding? The recipe for this dense, custardy version comes from one of our restaurants, Chez Nous. If we ever removed it from the menu, there would probably be a riot. It differs from most pot de crème recipes in that the custard is cooked only on the stovetop and not in the oven—that's what helps make it so satiny. This is a dessert you may not want to share, so enjoy it all by yourself. But take my advice, because I speak from personal experience: don't overdo it.

1. In a small bowl, whisk together the egg yolks and sugar. In a small saucepan, combine the heavy cream, vanilla bean and its scrapings, and salt and bring almost to a boil over medium heat. Just before the cream comes to a boil (the cream will start to rise up in the pan), remove from the heat and whisk 1 cup of the hot cream into the egg yolk mixture, then pour the tempered egg yolk mixture back into the pan with the remaining cream, whisking constantly. Discard the vanilla bean. Whisk the semisweet and bittersweet chocolates into the hot custard mixture until completely melted and smooth. Transfer custard to a medium bowl and refrigerate, whisking occasionally, until cooled to lukewarm and very thick. Pour the lukewarm, thickened custard into 8, 6-ounce ramekins. Cover and refrigerate until the custard is completely set, approximately 3 hours. Serve with softly whipped cream.

12 extra-large egg yolks

3/4 cup sugar

3 cups heavy cream

1/2 vanilla bean, split and scraped

1/4 teaspoon salt

4 ounces semisweet chocolate, finely chopped (approximately 2/3 cup)

4 ounces bittersweet chocolate, finely chopped (approximately 2/3 cup)

MAKES EIGHT 6-OUNCE RAMEKINS

ACKNOWLEDGMENTS

WRITING A BOOK LIKE THIS TURNS OUT TO BE just like opening a bakery or restaurant. It takes the dedication and passion of dozens of people, each doing their part, to make it all come together. Even if it isn't always immediately apparent, everyone involved contributes to the finished product. I'm so proud of what we've done and so grateful to all of you who have helped.

At Bay Bread, we are like a big family—one that happens to have several departments. I want to thank everyone in that family, including those who have worked with us in the past and left behind their recipes and personal touches, not only for the contributions you made, in the creation of this book, but also for your daily devotion to your work and to your Bay Bread "siblings."

Pastry

Keri Ramsay, the pastry chef of my heart, has passionately and patiently headed our pastry department from its beginning. Keri, you cried a lot, (usually right before I did), but I know you agree it was all worth it. Our amazing pastry chef Caroline Romanski carried us through the process and skillfully reworked many of the recipes for home baking. Sharon Saunders, pastry cook, mother of two and the world's most patient typist, tested and retested many of the recipes. Stefanie Cowan is a very talented pastry chef who loves to travel—please don't ever travel too far away. Jennifer Palmer is a gifted pastry chef with the highest standards—you laid the groundwork. Philippe Delarue is a master of the *macaron* and an existentialist—who also makes a mean rabbit in mustard sauce. Letty has blossomed into an excellent pastry cook and a real inspiration to us all—and what a smile! Daniel, it's great to have you with us . . . but what about those food costs? Gayle, you're wonderful, with a big heart—and I love that you love to bake. Thank you Carla and Christine—your cheerful dedication is a joy. Thank you Juanita, Julio, Oscar, William, Juan, Rogelio, and Eligio for all your hard work.

Bread

Elisio and Sergio, after seven years, your loyalty and talent mean a lot to me. *Gracias!* Jean-Jacques started "Bread Only!" in Los Angeles with Hubert and myself—and here you are now, baking with us again. Here's to you and here's to the good old days. Jean-Claude has the soul of the bakers that I baked with in France. Thank you Jose, Adan, Colli and Hugo.

Viennoiserie

Leonardo is the master of *Viennoiserie* and a great baker, as well. He is talented, smart and a loyal friend—sorry ladies, he's already married. My thanks to the entire *Viennoiserie* team: Daniel, Juan, Carlos, Honorio, Fidencio, and Miguel.

Retail

Sara Nakata was the soul of our Pine Street store. Sara, we miss you a lot. Clare Young-Wood is the new heart of the Boulangerie. Thank you Clare for your professionalism and integrity. You are just fantastic. Sophiene, we have enjoyed your sparkling personality since the beginning. Rudy, the customers love you, and we do too—try to leave the door open until 6:00 P.M., —just kidding! Thank you Ana, Susan, Anna, Gael, Samitha, Ajay, William, Michelle, and Caroline.

Thank you to Morgan, a great guy from the Southwest of France who reminds me every day of our beautiful countryside. Morgan, you are the soul of wholesome kindness.

To Nigel, Monique, Selvi, Pedro, Adrian, Erik, and Lucky; many thanks for the fantastic job you do taking care of our *Boulanges.*

Family on Wheels—Our Drivers

Magda and Violetta deliver our baked goods and work directly with our wonderful customers. You are the *joie de vivre* and courage on wheels. Thank you Hanssen, Sandra, and Constantin.

Our Chefs

Robert Cubberly was a tremendous help in setting up our *Boulange* stores. Thanks, Robert, for all you do and for your wonderful recipes. Marc Rasic, our young, talented chef—thank you for your collaboration and hard work. Thank you Francois Bernaudin, Edgar Pacheco, and Chris Fissel—thanks for contributing and for being such special people.

Special thank you to . . .

Alex, the mechanical genius who keeps every piece of equipment working around the clock; Elina and Lorraine who keep our office running smoothly; and Chou, contractor extraordinaire, we could never have grown so fast and so well without your building talents.

Floyd Yearout, who's love of food and search for authenticity led him to our Boulangerie door and who, with publisher James Connolly, first envisioned this book. Tina Salter, thank you for all your hard work in turning our recipes and the spirit of our boulangerie into a book— you know your book stuff, but even more important for me, you know and love great food. Photographer Paul Moore, stylist George Dolese and designer Catherine Jacobes, thanks for capturing that spirit in the beautiful, evocative images and pages you created. My thanks to Steve Siegelman for your creative wordsmithing, and Carolyn Krebs and Christine Swett for your careful editing and recipe revisions.

Monsieur Audouin, *boulanger et maire de Paillet,* thanks for giving me my start. I know you're watching from upstairs. Bernard Contraire, thanks for sharing your love of bread and your love of life. Michel Richard, you gave me my first chance in America, and I will always be grateful.

I want to send all my thanks to Kent, Pauline, the Perry Family, and Bob Payne for their tremendous support. Thank you, Al and Keith Giusto for helping along the way. Thank you Bob and Laurie Dennis for being our friends and for making legal sense of our perpetually rolling venture, and yes, the soaps are coming!

Olimpia—thank you for your warm love and devotion to our family.

And finally, a very special thank you to Lori Goodman, my partner in crime, *pour le meilleur et pour le pire,* for pulling this all together. We all love you dearly.

To all of you, from the bottom of my heart, *Merci Beaucoup.*

RESOURCES

The Baker's Catalogue
King Arthur Flour Company
P.O. Box 876
Norwich, Vermont 05055-0876
800-827-6836
www.bakerscatalogue.com

J.B. Prince Company, Inc.
36 East 31st Street
New York, New York 10016
800-473-0577
www.jbprince.com

Chef's Catalog
P.O. Box 620048
Dallas, Texas 75262-0048
800-338-3232
www.chefscatalog.com

IGO Foods
c/o Piperade
1015 Battery Street
San Francisco, California 94111
415-302-2323
www.piperade.com

Sur La Table
Catalog Division
P.O. Box 34707
Seattle, Washington 98124
800-243-0852
www.surlatable.com

Williams-Sonoma
Mail Order Department
P.O. Box 379900
Las Vegas, Nevada 89137
800-541-2233
www.williams-sonoma.com

Professional Cutlery Direct
242 Branford Road
North Branford, Connecticut 06471
800-859-6994
www.cutlery.com

INDEX

TABLE OF EQUIVALENTS

VOLUME MEASURES

U.S.	METRIC	IMPERIAL
$1/2$ teaspoon	2.5 milliliters	
1 teaspoon	5 milliliters	
1 tablespoon	15 milliliters	1 fluid ounce
$1/4$ cup	60 milliliters	2 fluid ounces
$1/3$ cup	75 milliliters	$2^1/2$ fluid ounces
$1/2$ cup	125 milliliters	4 fluid ounces
1 cup	250 milliliters	8 fluid ounces
2 cups (1 pint)	500 milliliters	16 fluid ounces
4 cups (1 quart)	1000 milliliters	32 fluid ounces

WEIGHT MEASURES

U.S.	METRIC
1 ounce	28 grams
4 ounces	112 grams
8 ounces	224 grams
1 pound	448 grams
2.2 pounds	1 kilogram

OVEN TEMPERATURES

FAHRENHEIT	CELSIUS	GAS
225	110	$1/4$
250	120	$1/2$
275	140	1
300	150	2
325	160	3
350	180	4
375	190	5
400	200	6
425	220	7
450	230	8
475	240	9